A Text Book of

HOSPITAL AND CLINICAL PHARMACY

SECOND YEAR DIPLOMA IN PHARMACY

D. J. PATIL
B. Pharm.
Institute of Pharmacy, Faizpur
Tal. Yawal, Dist. Jalgaon

HOSPITAL AND CLINICAL PHARMACY ISBN 978-81-85790-66-4

Sixth Edition : January 2016

© : Author

The text of this publication, or any part thereof, should not be reproduced or transmitted in any form or stored in any computer storage system or device for distribution including photocopy, recording, taping or information retrieval system or reproduced on any disc, tape, perforated media or other information storage device etc., without the written permission of Author with whom the rights are reserved. Breach of this condition is liable for legal action.

Every effort has been made to avoid errors or omissions in this publication. In spite of this, errors may have crept in. Any mistake, error or discrepancy so noted and shall be brought to our notice shall be taken care of in the next edition. It is notified that neither the publisher nor the author or seller shall be responsible for any damage or loss of action to any one, of any kind, in any manner, therefrom.

Published By :
NIRALI PRAKASHAN
Abhyudaya Pragati, 1312, Shivaji Nagar
Off J.M. Road, PUNE – 411005
Tel - (020) 25512336/37/39, Fax - (020) 25511379
Email : niralipune@pragationline.com

Printed By :
Repro Knowledgecast Limited,
Thane

DISTRIBUTION CENTRES

PUNE
- **Nirali Prakashan** : 119, Budhwar Peth, Jogeshwari Mandir Lane, Pune 411002, Maharashtra
  Tel : (020) 2445 2044, 66022708, Fax : (020) 2445 1538
  Email : bookorder@pragationline.com, niralilocal@pragationline.com
- **Nirali Prakashan** : S. No. 28/27, Dhyari, Near Pari Company, Pune 411041
  Tel : (020) 24690204 Fax : (020) 24690316
  Email : dhyari@pragationline.com, bookorder@pragationline.com

MUMBAI
- **Nirali Prakashan** : 385, S.V.P. Road, Rasdhara Co-op. Hsg. Society Ltd.,
  Girgaum, Mumbai 400004, Maharashtra
  Tel : (022) 2385 6339 / 2386 9976, Fax : (022) 2386 9976
  Email : niralimumbai@pragationline.com

DISTRIBUTION BRANCHES

JALGAON
- **Nirali Prakashan** : 34, V. V. Golani Market, Navi Peth, Jalgaon 425001,
  Maharashtra, Tel : (0257) 222 0395, Mob : 94234 91860

KOLHAPUR
- **Nirali Prakashan** : New Mahadvar Road, Kedar Plaza, 1st Floor Opp. IDBI Bank
  Kolhapur 416 012, Maharashtra. Mob : 9850046155

NAGPUR
- **Pratibha Book Distributors** : Above Maratha Mandir, Shop No. 3, First Floor,
  Rani Jhanshi Square, Sitabuldi, Nagpur 440012, Maharashtra
  Tel : (0712) 254 7129

DELHI
- **Nirali Prakashan** : 4593/21, Basement, Aggarwal Lane 15, Ansari Road, Daryaganj
  Near Times of India Building, New Delhi 110002
  Mob : 08505972553

BENGALURU
- **Pragati Book House** : House No. 1, Sanjeevappa Lane, Avenue Road Cross,
  Opp. Rice Church, Bengaluru – 560002.
  Tel : (080) 64513344, 64513355,Mob : 9880582331, 9845021552
  Email:bharatsavla@yahoo.com

CHENNAI
- **Pragati Books** : 9/1, Montieth Road, Behind Taas Mahal, Egmore,
  Chennai 600008 Tamil Nadu, Tel : (044) 6518 3535,
  Mob : 94440 01782 / 98450 21552 / 98805 82331,
  Email : bharatsavla@yahoo.com

niralipune@pragationline.com | www.pragationline.com
Also find us on www.facebook.com/niralibooks

PREFACE TO THE SIXTH EDITION

It is indeed an honour to the Sixth revised edition of text book **Hospital and Clinical Pharmacy** on successful completion of Second and Third Editions.

The wide acceptance and popularity of previous edition of the book have encouraged me to bring about the next edition.

In recent times there has been vast accumulation of knowledge on pharmacy practices. So there is emphasis on the patient care and pharmaceutical care rendered to the health community, to fulfill the needs of new millenrium pharmacists.

It is a pleasure to thank all those who have made useful suggestions for improvement. I am must grateful to my publisher Shri. Jigneshbhai Furia for getting this edition through the press.

Deelip J. Patil

DEDICATED TO

Shri. Avadhutanand Maharaj
&
My Father, Mother and Sister

SYLLABUS

HOSPITAL AND CLINICAL PHARMACY

PART – I : HOSPITAL PHARMACY

1. Hospitals : Definition, Function, Classifications based on various criteria, organisation, management and health delivery system in India.

2. Hospital Pharmacy :
   (a) Definition
   (b) Functions and objectives of Hospital Pharmaceutical services.
   (c) Location, Layout, Flow chart of materials and men.
   (d) Personnel and facilities requirements including equipment's based on individual and basic needs.
   (e) Requirements and abilities required for Hospital Pharmacists.

3. Drug Distribution system in Hospitals :
   (a) Out-patient services
   (b) In-patient services :
       (i) Types of services
       (ii) Detailed discussion of Unit dose system, Floor ward stock system, Satellite pharmacy services, Central sterile services, Bed Side Pharmacy

4. Manufacturing :
   (a) Economical considerations estimation of demand.
   (b) Sterile manufacture, large and small volume parenterals, facilities, requirements, layout, production planning, man-power requirements.
   (c) Non-sterile manufacture – Liquid orals, Externals, Bulk concentrates.
   (d) Procurement of stores and testing of raw materials.

5. Nomenclature and uses of surgical instruments and Hospital Equipments and health accessories.

6. P.T.C. (Pharmacy Therapeutic Committee), Hospital Formulary System and their organisation, functioning, composition.

7. Drug Information service and Drug Information Bulletin.

8. Surgical dressing like cotton, gauze, bandages and adhesive tapes including their pharmacopoeial test for quality. Other hospital supply e.g. I.V. sets, B.T. sets, Rypes tubes, Catheters, Syringes, etc.

9. Application of computers in maintenance of records, inventory control, medication monitoring, drug information and data storage and retrieval in hospital and retail pharmacy establishments.

PART – II : CLINICAL PHARMACY

1. Introduction to Clinical Pharmacy Practice – Definition, Scope.
2. Modern dispensing aspects - Pharmacists and Patient counselling and advice for the use of common drugs, medication history.
3. Common daily terminology used in the Practice of Medicine.
4. Disease, manifestations and pathophysiology including salient symptoms to understand the diseases like Tuberculosis, Hepatitis, Rheumatoid Arthritis, Cardio-Vascular diseases, Epilepsy, Diabetes, Peptic Ulcer, Hypertension.
5. Physiological parameters with their significance.
6. Drugs interactions :
    (a) Definition and introduction.
    (b) Mechanism of Drug interaction.
    (c) Drug-drug interaction with reference to analgesics, diuretics, cardio vascular drugs. Gastro-intrestinal agent Vitamins and Hypoglycemic agents.
    (d) Drug-food interaction.
7. Adverse Drug Reactions.
    (a) Definition and significance.
    (b) Drug - induced diseases and Teratogenicity.
8. Drugs in Clinical Toxicity - Introduction, general treatment of poisoning, systematic antidotes. Treatment insecticide poisoning heavy metal poisoning, Narcotic drugs, Barbiturate, Organophosphorus poisons.
9. Drug dependance, Drug abuse, Addicive drugs and their treatment complications.
10. Bio-availability of drugs, including factors affecting it.

•••

CONTENTS

PART – I : HOSPITAL PHARMACY

1.	HOSPITALS	1.1 – 1.14
2.	HOSPITAL PHARMACY	2.1 – 2.8
3.	DRUG DISTRIBUTION SYSTEM IN HOSPITALS	3.1 – 3.10
4.	PROCUREMENT OF STORES AND INVENTORY CONTROL	4.1 – 4.6
5.	HOSPITAL MANUFACTURING	5.1 – 5.24
6.	SURGICAL INSTRUMENTS, MEDICAL EQUIPMENTS AND HEALTH ACCESSORIES	6.1 – 6.12
7.	PHARMACY AND THERAPEUTIC COMMITTEE AND HOSPITAL FORMULARY	7.1 – 7.6
8.	DRUG INFORMATION SERVICES AND DRUG INFORMATION BULLETIN	8.1 – 8.4
9.	SURGICAL DRESSINGS AND SUPPLIES	9.1 – 9.14
10.	COMPUTERS	10.1 – 10.4

PART – II : CLINICAL PHARMACY

1.	INTRODUCTION TO CLINICAL PHARMACY	1.1 – 1.4
2.	MODERN DISPENSING ASPECTS	2.1 – 2.6
3.	MEDICAL TERMINOLOGY	3.1 – 3.8
4.	DISEASES, MANIFESTATIONS AND SYMPTOMS	4.1 – 4.14
5.	PHYSIOLOGICAL PARAMETERS	5.1 – 5.14
6.	DRUG INTERACTIONS	6.1 – 6.8
7.	ADVERSE DRUG REACTIONS	7.1 – 7.8
8.	DRUGS IN CLINICAL TOXICITY	8.1 – 8.14
9.	DRUG DEPENDENCE	9.1 – 9.6
10.	BIO-AVAILABILITY OF DRUGS	10.1 – 10.4

•••

ACKNOWLEDGEMENT

By publishing this book at Nirali Prakashan, PUNE. I have received a "devine gift" from Shri. Dineshbhai Furia and Shri. Jigneshbhai Furia.

I would like to thanks Professor-cum-Author Chitode Janardan S. and his Publisher brothers Avinash and Ravi Wani (Technical Publication, PUNE) for taking keen interest and guiding me in writing this book.

Lastly I should be failing in my duty if I do not express my gratitude to Shri. "Lok-Sevak" - Madhukar-rao Chaudhari (Ex. President of Vidhan-Sabha, Maharashtra State Govt.), My Principal, Colleagues and especially my Wife and Son Reesh.

•••

PREFACE TO THE FIRST EDITION

कर्मण्येवाधिकारस्ते मा पफलेषु कदाचन !
मा कर्मपफलहेतुर्भू मा ते संगोस्त्व कर्मणि स्त्वकर्मणि !!

You must do your job, but not a right on its reward. Don't do the job with an aim of gain and avoid the company of those who drawback.

Today in India the status of community pharmacy is in the primitive stage and is confined to the so called "Medical Store". The successful, fulfilling role of community pharmacist is yet to be recognised.

Hence I take privilege to give a comprehensive book on the subject namely "Hospital and Clinical Pharmacy" for the second year D. Pharm. Students.

The text of this book has been prepared exactly as per ER-91 in a simple and lucid language.

I truely look for ward to appreciate my efforts and enthusiasm. I would always welcome to healthy criticisms, comments and guidance with reference to the first edition.

My specials thanks to Shri. Jigneshbhai Furia, Publisher of Nirali Books Pvt. Ltd., Pune for getting the book through the press.

Deelip J. Patil

PART I : HOSPITAL PHARMACY

1

HOSPITALS

(The Life Savers)

INTRODUCTION

Hospital is a very complex organisation with a specific aim of restoration and maintenance of good health. It provides special facilities like nursing, dietary, blood banking, patient counselling and skilled personnels and team of physicians and surgeons for patient care.

In 1986 WHO (World Health Organisation) formed the Global Programme Committee. Committee adopted a concept of District Health System, which is based on primary healthcare and is a part of our national health policy.

DEFINITION

Hospital is defined as an institution that provides community health, where diagnosis therapy, rehabilitation, training and social services are provided.

HISTORY OF HOSPITALS

Perhaps the archaeology section of Hindu temples started a very small bed size hospital. It was looked after by few doctors, who were given a small piece of land or paddy for the services they provided. Diseases like Asthma, fever dropsy, pile and jaundice were treated in those hospitals.

Later on Ayurveda, Unani-Siddha and Homeopathic types of medicines were adopted by the Doctors and Hakims who used to visit villages and patients at their homes. As we are in millennium 2000, advancement of medical science and technology in diagnostic and surgical area will certainly help to build up confidence to render better service to the community to ensure good health.

FUNCTIONS OF MODERN HOSPITAL

1. **Patient care :** It includes services for diagnosis, prophylaxis and treatment of diseases to the patients. The in-patient services are equally important by providing hospitalisation facility.

2. **Immunisation :** It helps to prevent the disease. A small unit is run in an OPD section, where children are immunised by giving different vaccines like B.C.G, Hepatitis, Small pox etc.

3. **Counselling and Patient advice :** It is a modern concept adopted in big hospitals for the well-being of the patients. During these counselling sessions pharmacist educate people on communicable diseases, epidemics and family welfare, etc.

4. **Coordination :** Especially, hospitals that run under the control of the Government act as interlinks between the health policies and the general public. The District hospitals deal with urban and primary health centres.

5. **Rehabilitation :** This facility is provided to drug addicts, chronic alcoholics and psychiatric patients by specific therapy and supportive measures like "Yoga" and advice.

6. **Research :** This should be a vital function of hospital to contribute to the advancement of medical knowledge against diseases and improvement of hospital services in order to render better patient care. This includes devising new diagnostic procedures and techniques.

7. **Educational Training :** This facility, particularly for medical students, pharmacists, nursing, medical technologists and allied health professionals helps to fulfill their curriculum requirement.

8. **Workshop and Seminar :** Such activity is arranged periodically at state level conferences or in the hospitals to furnish the details of recent studies or *acute syndromes* like SARS (Severe Acute Respiratory Syndrome).

Concept of District Hospital

The district hospital is a constitutional health and family welfare policy of the nation. A district hospital has to manage all the needs of the district population.

The district hospital provides clinical service, clinical and non-clinical support including administrative services.

(a) **Clinical service :** This is a prime and vital need of the patients. This could be provided via various medicinal divisions like gynaecology, pediatric, cardiac, orthopeadic etc.

(b) **Clinical support :** Services like pathology, radiology, blood bank, anaesthesia provide significant support to a physician while diagnosing the disease or conducting surgery.

(c) **Non-clinical support :** This also plays an important role in well-being of the patient. This is provided as a part of the services to the customer. For example, catering, linen and house keeping.

(d) **Administrative services :** These are needed for the smooth functioning of the hospitals. This include finance, personnel, maintaining medical records and pursuing legal matter, procurement, of medicines providing security etc.

Classification of hospitals :

There are number of criteria by which the hospitals could be classified. They could be *clinical* and *non-clinical*-oriented.

(A) Clinical - oriented : These are again further classified on a different basis :

  (a) On the basis of type of medicine used to cure the disease :
    (i) Allopathic hospitals
    (ii) Ayurvedic hospitals
    (iii) Siddha and Unani hospitals
    (iv) Homeopathic hospitals
    (v) Physiotherapy centres

  (b) On the basis of Anatomy and Physiology
    (i) ENT hospitals
    (ii) Cardiac centres
    (iii) Eye hospitals
    (iv) Kidney hospitals
    (v) Orthopaedic hospitals
    (vi) Neurological hospitals

  (c) On the basis of type of patients
    (i) General hospitals
    (ii) Gynaecology and maternity hospitals
    (iii) Paediatric hospitals
    (iv) Psychiatric hospitals
    (v) Accident hospitals
    (vi) Rehabilitation centres (for drug addicts)

  (d) On the basis of disease
    (i) Cancer hospitals
    (ii) T.B. hospitals
    (iii) Leprosy hospitals
    (iv) Diabetes hospitals

  (e) On the basis of objective
    (i) General hospitals e.g. PHCs, Municipality.
    (ii) Special hospitals e.g. Cancer, T.B., Dental.
    (iii) Teaching and Research Hospitals. e.g. AIIMS - New Delhi.

(B) Non-Clinical-Oriented Hospitals :

These types of hospitals are run under the control of various bodies, cost, bed size and are classified as :

1. **Ownership basis :**

    (a) **Controlled by the Central Government**
      (i) Military Hospitals
      (ii) Railway Hospitals
      (iii) All India Institute of Medical Sciences, New Delhi.
      (iv) JIPMER Hospital, Pondicherry.

    (b) **Controlled by State Government**
      (i) J.J. Hospital – Mumbai
      (ii) Sassoon Hospital – Pune
      (iii) Ghati Hospital – Aurangabad
      (iv) ESI Hospital – Mulund (Mumbai)
      (v) Victoria Hospital – Bengaluru
      (vi) Stanley Hospital – Chennai
      (vii) Civil Hospital – Jalgaon.

    (c) **Controlled by Corporation / Municipality**
      (i) BMC Hospital – Sion, Mumbai
      (ii) KEM Hospital – Parel, Mumbai
      (iii) Cooper Hospital – Vile Parle, Mumbai
      (iv) Bhagwati Hospital – Mumbai.

    (d) **Private Trust Hospitals**
      (i) Bombay Hospital – Marine lines, Mumbai
      (ii) Jaslok Hospital – Mumbai
      (iii) Rajasthan Hospital – Ahmedabad
      (iv) Jindal Hospital – Bengaluru

    (e) **Run by religious bodies :**
      (i) Hindu Mission Hospital – Chennai
      (ii) Al-Ameen Hospital – Bengaluru
      (iii) Christian Medical College Hospital – Vellore
      (iv) Minakshi Mission Hospital – Madurai.

(f) **Public Limited Company Hospitals**
  (i) Wokhardt Hospital – Bengaluru
  (ii) Apollo Hospital – Chennai
  (iii) Medinovo Hospital – Gujarat
  (iv) HMT Hospital – Hyderabad

(g) **Private Clinics / nursing homes :** Such clinics are owned by an individual doctor or a group of doctors in towns or big cities and serve for 24 hrs.

2. **On the basis of cost :**

   (a) **Costly hospitals :**

   e.g. (i) Breach Candy Hospital, (ii) Jaslok Hospital.

   (b) **Low budget hospitals :**

   e.g. Civil and Corporation hospitals.

   (c) **Free/Conventional cost hospitals :**

   e.g. Manilal Kantilal Hospital, Ahmedabad.

3. **On the basis of bed size :**

   (a) **Large hospitals :** The bed size is more than 1000.

   e.g. J.J. and K.E.M. hospitals.

   (b) **Medium hospitals :** The bed size is in between 500 - 1000.

   e.g. Jaslok and Bombay hospitals.

   (c) **Small hospitals :** The bed size lies in the range of 500 - 100.

   e.g. Breach Candy Hospital.

   (d) **Very small hospitals :** The bed size is less then 100.

   e.g. Municipal hospitals and private clinics.

4. **Hospital attached to medical colleges :**

   e.g. Pravra Medical College, Bharti Vidyapeeth's Medical College.

ORGANISATION OF HOSPITALS

Hospitals are complex institutions dealing with not only patient care but also involved in R & D and professional education. Their main objective is to provide quality health care.

Like an Industry, hospital is an unique place where patients of all ages and background interact with physicians, therapists, pharmacists, nurses, pathologists and administrators. Therefore, the organisational structure depends upon the activities going around the patient.

A proposed set up of organisation of hospital is an under :

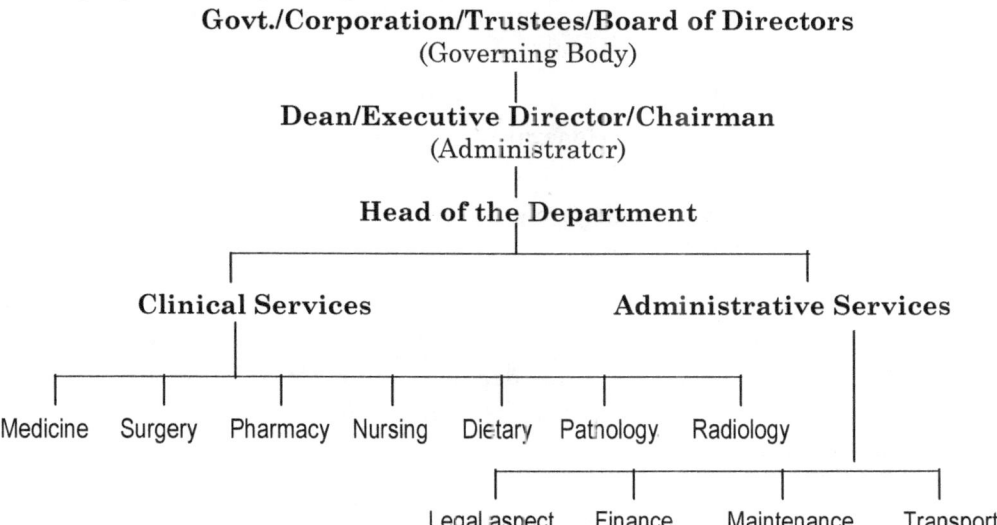

Governing body comprises the legal status to the hospital, which is in the form of society, trust or board of directors. The governing body is overall responsible for the proper functioning of the hospital and the services rendered to the patient. An executive director or a chair-person is appointed as an **administrator**.

The **administrator** is assisted by the down line professionals and experts in their respective fields. He is an interlink between the medical staff and the governing body. He is responsible :

1. For implementing the policies laid down by the body.
2. He forms some committees on an adhoc basis, like professional committee, finance, purchase and other.
3. The administrator looks after the availability of medical staff to ensure proper medical care to the patients.

The medical staff is categorised on the basis of working.

1. **Residential Medical Officer (R.M.O.)** : He is a residential medical officer, who is available on a 24 hours service basis to attend the patients under any circumstances.
2. **Consultants** : These are expert medical practitioners in specific segments of medicines. They come to the hospital on a particular day and time to provide consultation to the needy.
3. **Visiting specialist** : He is also an expert in a specific branch of medicine. He practices in his own clinic. He is called on by the hospital to attend the emergency cases or to give his expert opinion on any special case.
4. **Honorary staff** : Generally they are retired medical professionals. They provide honorary services to the hospital besides their private practice as consultants or surgeons.

5. Head of the Department (HOD) : Competent, experienced and expert, in his own branch of medicine, is appointed as HOD of the department, and is a full-time salarised professional.

There are different Departments that can be formed as under :

1. **Medicine Divisions :** General medicine, Gynaecology, Paediatrics cardiology, Neurology and Psychiatry etc.
2. **Surgery Divisions :** General surgery, obstetric and gynaecology, opthalmalogy, orthopaedic etc.

Functions of HOD :

1. He is overall responsible for the activities going on in his Department.
2. He fulfills the requirements in his department and looks after the quality of services being provided to the patients by his division.
3. He prepares the budget for his division for future plan. He also arranges workshops of educational programmes for his department.
4. He prepares and submits the monthly report of his division to the administrator of the hospital.

The Clinical Departments :

The number of departments of clinical services of the hospital depends upon the specialised medical staff. Generally, the services offered by the hospital could be summarised as medicine, surgery, pathology, radiology including supportive services like dietary, house-keeping and linen.

Services like nursing, blood banking and pharmacy have their own significant value in healthcare system of the hospital.

Surgical Division :

The major population from the patient category may have to undergo surgery for restoration of health. Professionally skilled surgeons render these services. Utilising the advanced techniques and sophisticated instruments, a particular organ or a body system is operated upon by a specialist surgeon like neurosurgeon, cardiovascular surgeon, dental and oral surgeon etc.

Besides the surgeon, this division requires an anaesthetist to anaesthetize the patient before the surgery. The nursing staff and chief of operation theatre assist in functioning of the division.

To operate the patient a hospital needs an Operation Theatre (O.T.), which should have a sterile environment. It should be well designed and equipped with vital instruments, surgical accessories and sufficient amount of illumination facility.

The central sterile services takes care of the supply of articles like sterilised surgical instruments, ligature and sutures including cotton wool, gauze etc.

Radiology :

Radiology is a branch of medicine, which deals with diagnostic and therapeutic value as well. This division generally comprises of a radiologist, therapists, who are assisted by a physicist and technicians.

Big hospitals have modern, advanced and computer-aided instruments like C.T. scan, sonography and CAT (Computer-Aided Tomography).

A Radiologist or Radiation safety committee looks after the safe use and proper handling of radio-isotope substances needed for X-ray screening, radiology an fluoroscopy.

Maternity :

This is one of the basic facilities provided to the community by the hospitals. Even in rural areas the hospitals conduct deliveries. All the procedures of maternity and delivery units are followed. Proper records, such as infants record, birth record, are properly maintained and the Govt. authorities are informed.

Special provisions such as new born infants care, pre-mature infant services and feeding are also available.

Clinical and Pathology Services :

Now-a-days the scenario of diagnosis has changed. It is clinical and pathological orientated rather than symphomatic, even for diseases like Typhoid and Malaria. Apart from this, some of the body systems are gauged by certain parameters like Haematogram, cholesterol and blood glucose level etc. The change in normal values indicates abnormality or disfunction due to disorder/ disease.

This is a separate entity working in a hospital, headed by the M.D. Pathologist, and is assisted by physicist and technicians. It comprises sections like haematology, Histocytopathology, Serology, Biochemistry and pathophysiology. Each section is well-designed and equipped as per the norms laid down by the Govt. authority.

General facilities such as waiting room, blood testing area, toilet and auxiliary are provided.

Blood Bank :

The FDA has declared blood as a therapeutic agent. Therefore, these services need a separate licence to function. This is a very modern laboratory technology with availability of all the instruments required for collection, processing, testing and storage.

A separate room is required for maintenance of donor records, testing records and stock register of day-to-day working.

M.D. Haematologist is the head of the unit supported by a physicist and technicians, including a micro-biologist.

Blood as a whole as well as its active constituents has therapeutic value. Now-a-days a threat of diseases like AIDS, STD and other infectious diseases (T.B., Hepatitis etc.) is taken into account apart from ABO grouping and Rh factor.

The blood bank procedure can be understood as follows :

1. **Receiving and Examination of Donor :** A complete registry of donor is taken as : Name, address, sex, body weight and a brief query about medical history.

2. **Collecting, Processing and Storage of blood :** Blood is collected by venepuncture method in a container, which contains a anticoagulant like Acid-Citrate-Dextrose and then it is stored at 4°C in cold storage. It remains stable for 21 days at 1 - 6°C.

3. **ABO grouping and compatability testing before transfusion :** A sample of donors blood is tested for ABO and Rh factor and it is categorised accordingly. At the same time serological tests are performed for HIV, Hepatitis etc. Finally, the container is labelled with all details.

NURSING SERVICES

Nursing is a vital prime need of the health care system of a hospital. It involves numerous activities, ranging from general assistance to out-patients to the in-patient area and wards, Labour wards and O.T. (Operation Theatre).

It is one of the largest and an integral part of the hospital, performing round the clock duty. Similarly, to medical division the nursing services has clinical specialities like medical, surgical, obstetric, intensive care etc.

The administrator of these services is known as **H.O.D. or superintendent** of nursing. She is overall responsible for the activities of the department, by virtue of her administrative ability. The responsibilities are summarised as :

1. Coordination with all other departments, and allotment of nurses required in all the shifts.

2. Sending monthly reports regarding the activities of her own services to the Director of the hospital.

3. Maintaining nursing records and quality of services given to the patient.

4. Looking after the needs of her department staff and arranging training programmes for them including fellow nurses.

In case of ICU and ICCU unit a specific number of nurses are posted. She attends to an individual patient, closely monitoring and handling sophisticated equipments.

Apart from the above functions, nursing involves administration of medicine, prescribed by the physicians to the in-patients.

Importance of Nursing Services :

Nursing is the only services which runs round the clock in a hospital for patient care. Therefore, the importance can be summarised as :

1. **For Ambulatory patients :** Basically, these are the patient, who do not occupy the bed in a hospital. Despite this the nursing services helps them by :

    (a) **Preparation of case paper :** When the patient comes to the hospital, at the registration counter the case paper is prepared by the duty nurse.

    (b) **Guide to the patient :** Once the case paper is prepared she guide the patient for to whom he suppose to consult for getting the treatment.

    (c) **Assistance to the physician :** Whatever the judgement obtained after diagnosis mentioned in case paper is explained to the patient regarding the course of treatment to be followed.

2. **For Inpatients :** These patient stays in a hospital for maintenance and restoration of normal health or surgery.

    (a) **Patient care :** Collectively, it comprises the following services :

    (i) Checking of normograms, routinely such as body temperature, B.P., pulse rate etc.

    (ii) Administration of medicine as per schedule.

    (iii) Overall monitoring of patient's status and conveys it to the physician.

    (b) **For operating patients :** The services can be summarised as :

    (i) The patient is prepared before surgery in context of checking the essential physiological parameters.

    (ii) Consult pharmacy and administration department to obtain O.T. requirement such as sterile articles and anesthetist respectively.

    (iii) She prepare O.T. with respect to arrangement of equipment, surgical instruments and supplies.

    (iv) She monitor the patient condition continuously in O.T. during critical hours.

MEDICAL RECORDS

Medical record is a complete documented data of a patient. It includes patients admission slip, medical history, physical examination report, clinical/pathological tests reports, X-ray or other radiological examination reports, diagnosis report, therapy given, a letter of consent in case of surgery, anaesthesia record, discharge details and further check-up reports. The medical record furnishes the following details, which could be used for follow-up purposes :

1. It could be used for research as a case study.

2. It is an important record for legal purposes.

3. It gives a complete medical history of the patient.
4. It helps in evaluation of adverse drug reactions produced by idiosyncrasy.
5. The retrieval of data regarding mortality rate and birth rate becomes easier.

Dietary Services :

The services are headed by a well-qualified personnel known as dietitian. He shall be well-versed with the principles of nutritional science.

A menu of food served to the patients depends upon the following factors :

1. The type of disorder and condition of the patient.
2. Drugs are being given to the patients, (Food drug interaction) it may alter absorption of drugs.
3. Patient on restricted diet.
4. Calories needed to the patient.
5. Food allergies, etc.

The Dietitian is responsible for the supply of food and cup of coffee/tea to the medical staff and other personnel working in a hospital. He plans and accordingly purchases the foodgrains, vegetables, fruits and milk tins.

HOUSE KEEPING

It is a service rendered by the administrative department, which helps in the well-being of the patient. Now-a-days hygiene is being a part of supportive services, eliciting psychological advantage to the health care system. House keeping involves the activities as summarised below :

1. Dry cleaning of floor and corridors, followed by mopping with a suitable antiseptic solution.
2. Preparation of beds by changing bed sheets and blankets.
3. Removal of trash and other disposable items.
4. Replacement of sputum tray and urine bottles.
5. Cleaning of window grills.
6. Maintenance of toilet.

Sewage and it's disposal :

Sewage is a waste, may be liquid or soft solid in nature, generated by the community, and the methods by which it is disposed off is called as sewerage system.

Sewerage is a very complex activity, including preliminary screening by which the solid is separated by sedimentation or filtration. Plastic items like disposable surgical supplies (syringes, I.V. set, B.D. set, B.T. set) are segregated from other solid wastes.

Selection of disposal system depends on the nature and properties like physical, chemical and biological properties of the waste. To set up or design the system following data must be studied.

1. A complete analysis of sewage.
2. An estimate of the amount of sewage that may be generated.
3. The method, by which it may be disposed off.

Operation Theatre (O.T.), canteen, wards and laundry are the major sources, that generate the sewage of different natures. Solid waste is mostly generated by O.T. and wards, whereas liquid by laundry and canteen.

Raw waste consists of organic and inorganic materials which could be decomposed by :

1. **Aerobic bacteria :** which needs oxygen for survival.
2. **Anaerobic bacteria :** carbondioxide favours their growth.
3. **Facultative bacteria :** can survive in absence of oxygen under a favourable conditions the sewage get decomposed itself. The process is carried out by the following ways :

    (a) In septic tanks the waste is stored for a defined period of time, to allow anaerobic bacteria to act on it. Then the decomposed waste is disposed off by percolation in the ground.

    (b) Lagooning, in which small ponds or lakes are prepared and the waste is exposed to the atmosphere and sunlight. It allows the aerobic bacteria to decompose.

The effluent produced can be utilised for soil conditioning as a compose fertilizer or fish culture, because of its valuable constituents formed during the process of decomposition.

Disposal of Solid waste :

It comprises, cotton, wool, bandages, plasters and other garbages. Apart from plastic disposable items, all other solid waste is subjected to an **incinerator.**

The plastic items, syringes and I.V. sets are subjected for grinding in cutter mill and then those granules are sold to plastic industries for the fabrication of domestic articles.

HEALTH DELIVERY SYSTEM IN INDIA

It is a very vital aspect in our constitution. Union Ministry of Heath and Family Welfare is framed in the Central Government.

The Union Ministry formulates the policies and schemes regarding health and welfare programmes. The finance ministry provides funds by planning in the annual budget. The assistance is provided to the State Govt. in all the schemes rendered by it.

The schematic system of Health delivery in India at union and state level is summarised as below:

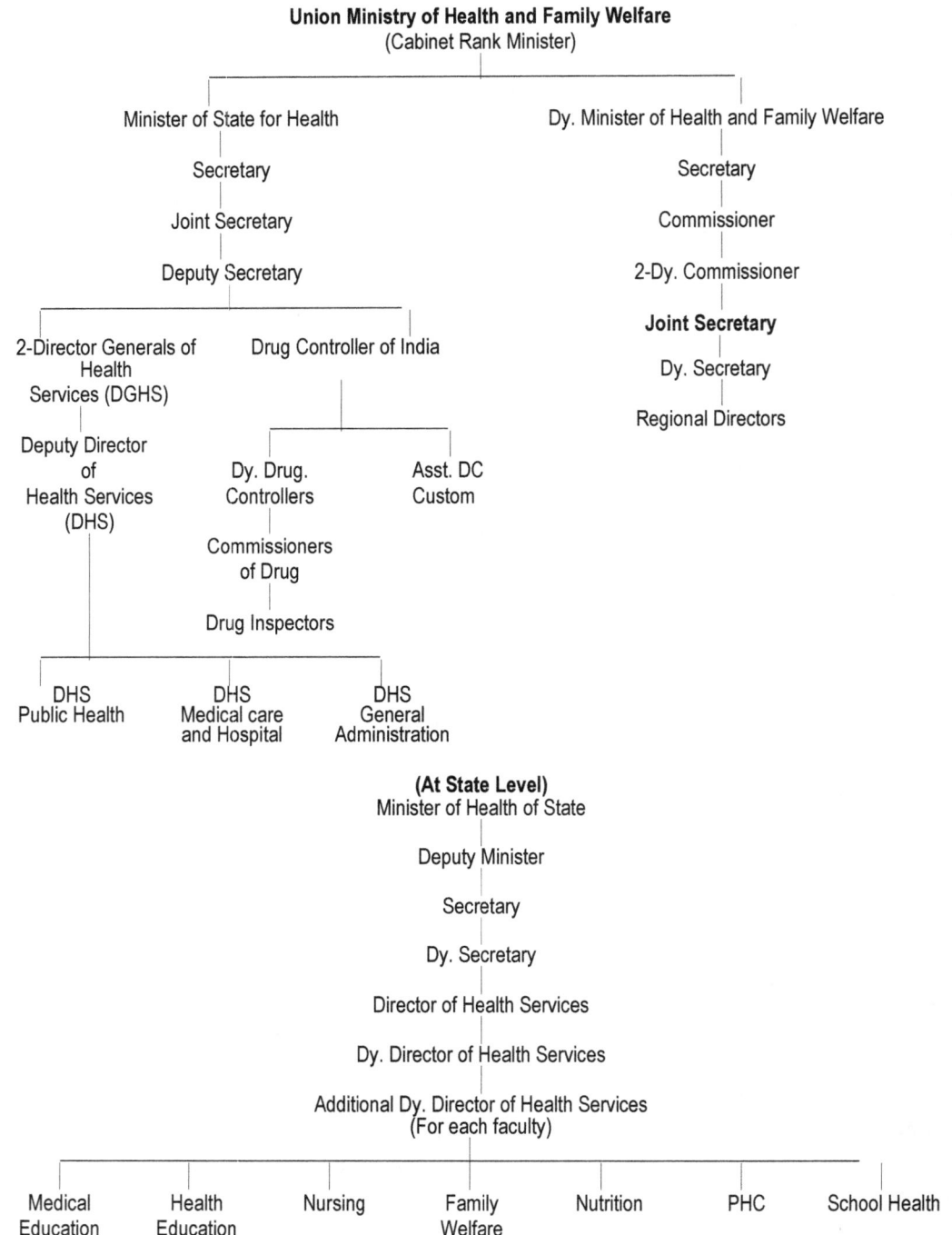

QUESTIONS

1. Define the term hospital and classify them on different basis.
   (W - 00, S - 01, S - 04, S - 96, S - 97)
2. Explain the various functions and objectives of modern hospital.
   (W - 97, 98, 00, S - 96, 97, 99)
3. Describe the organisation of hospital.
4. Write types of medical staff and give the functions of H.O.D.
5. What is sewage ? How it is disposed off ? Explain in brief.
6. Give an account of the health delivery system in India. **(S - 01, 04)**
7. Who is the administrator of Hospital ? Write its responsibility. **(W - 96)**
8. Write short notes on :
   (a) Radiology
   (b) Nursing
   (c) Clinical labs
   (d) Blood bank
   (e) House-keeping
   (f) Medical records.

2

HOSPITAL PHARMACY

(The Backbone)

INTRODUCTION

Hospital pharmacy is a department that provides pharmaceutical services to the outdoor and the indoor patients. The department is headed by a professionally competent and legally qualified (Registered) pharmacist.

Professional competency means the person with adequate knowledge and skill to manage the departmental activities alongwith the services to be rendered to the patient. The prime objective of the hospital's pharmaceutical services is to provide safe and effective medicines to all the patients, attending the hospital or the clinic. The services must be safe, efficient and economical.

DEFINITION

Hospital pharmacy may be defined as a department of a hospital. Wherein procurement, storage, compounding, dispensing or distribution is done under a control of a legally qualified pharmacist.

OBJECTIVES OF THE HOSPITAL PHARMACY

The objectives are designed to fulfill the legal aspects mentioned under the Pharmacy Act 1945 and execute them for the following purposes.

1. To render the services in a professional manner.
2. To work with ethics and follow the code of conduct on hospital pharmacy.
3. To implement the policies and standards laid down by the Pharmacy Therapeutic Committee.
4. To act as a counselling centre of furnish information to the patients, nursing and follow staff.
5. To improve and strengthen the scientific, technical, management skills and GMP/GLP practices for providing better services.
6. To ensure regular supply of medicines at reasonable rates.
7. To co-ordinate and co-operate effectively with other departments of the hospital.
8. To appoint skilled and trained registered pharmacist to serve in the hospital.

FUNCTIONS OF HOSPITAL PHARMACY

Numerous activities are performed in a hospital pharmacy under the supervision of the head pharmacist. These are summarised as under:

(A) Pharmacy Activities:

They include:

1. Procurement of drugs and medicines and their proper storage.
2. Compounding of drugs and dispensing them to out patients on the prescription of the physician of a hospital.
3. Distribution of drugs/medicine to indoor patients through wards.
4. Arranging bulk supplies to mini pharmacy, satellite pharmacy and unit-dose dispensing units operating in a hospital.
5. Providing facility to store narcotics and poisonous drugs separately and maintaining its record properly.

(B) Supportive activities:

Apart from pharmacy functions, the hospital pharmacy helps other departments in multiple ways:

1. It purchases, stores and supplies ancillary items and articles needed in the hospital.
2. Hospital pharmacy counsels patients on prescribed drugs, especially to out-patients.
3. It maintains detailed accounts of purchases, receipts and supply of drugs and medicines and furnishes them to the accounts department.

(C) Educational activities:

The hospital pharmacy renders educative services to the staff of the hospital and pharmacy professionals.

1. It provides information on new drugs, technology and products etc. to the doctors and maintains it in the library.
2. It carries out drug monitoring by studying the effects of drugs given to the In-patients; and maintains the data in the Drug Information Centre.
3. Arranges Seminars, workshops on topics like sterilization, medication errors, patient compliance etc. for nursing and newly appointed pharmacist.
4. Provides training facilities for fellow pharmacists.

LOCATION AND LAYOUT OF HOSPITAL PHARMACY

The hospital pharmacy should be located in such a place that it is convenient for it to provide services to all other concerned departments on a daily basis.

Generally the hospital pharmacy is located either in the ground or the first floor, adjacent to the out-patient department. This facilitates efficiency.

The out-patient pharmacy must look decent with enough space for the waiting patients with adequate seating facility. A notice board may be fixed or provision may be made to paste posters on health education, family planning, hygiene etc.

While designing the pharmacy, the following factors should be kept in mind.

1. **It must be located in such a place that :**
   (a) It is easily accessible to the out-patient department.
   (b) Dispensing becomes feasible and economical.
   (c) It is convenient to the central delivery department.
2. **The size should be determined by its operational activities.**
3. **Provisions should be made for :**
   (a) Washing of containers of equipments.
   (b) Storage of bulk solutions and concentrates.
   (c) Storage of poisonous and narcotic drugs.
   (d) Adequate seating facility for staff.
   (e) Fire control.

Typical Layout of a hospital Pharmacy

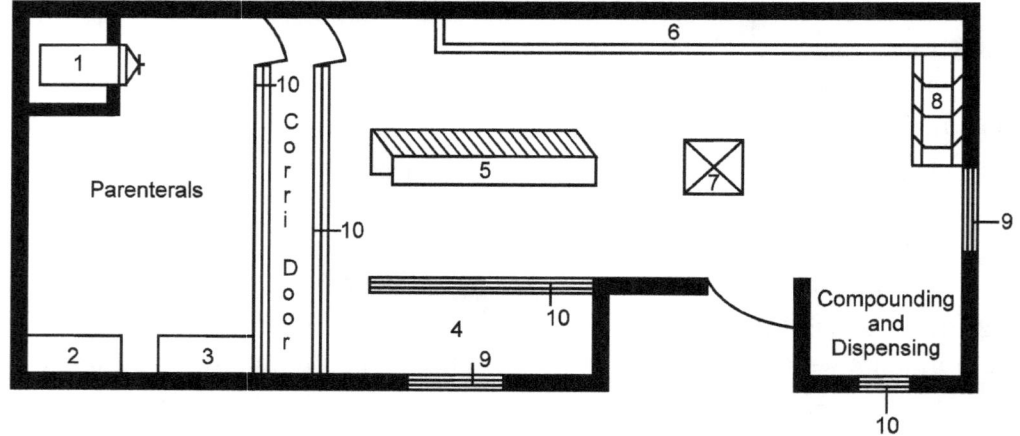

1. Sterilizer
2. Water system
3. Container area
4. Active medicament
5. Working station
6. Rack (storage)
7. Seating
8. Filing Rack
9. Glass window
10. Glass Partition

Requirements of the Hospital Pharmacy

Apart from the rules specified under the Drug and Cosmetic Act 1945, according to Schedule M and N a pharmacy needs floor space and personnel for its smooth functioning. The facilities needed are grouped as under :

(A) Floor space requirement :

The specified floor space required for different activities of the Hospital pharmacy is given in table Number 2.1.

Table 2.1

Sr. No.	Activity	50 beds	100 beds	200 beds
		Minimum area required in sq. ft. based on bed capacity		
1.	Compounding and Dispensing	205	320	495
2.	Parenteral preparation	–	185	200
3.	Store Room	–	125	200
4.	Manufacturing area	–	–	120
5.	Office and Library	–	–	105
6.	Circulation	–	–	60
	Total	205	630	1180

(B) Equipments requirement :

Like floor space, Schedule M of the Drug and Cosmetic Act 1945 specifies requirements of machinery for various dosage from manufacturing sections. These are minimum requirements and a guide line only.

While selecting equipment for a hospital pharmacy one must ensure :
(i) How to provide good services with minimum cost.
(ii) How the services could be provided efficiently.

Generally the hospital pharmacy equipment are classified into :

(a) Fixed equipment : Are the equipment, installed with the building during construction :
  e.g. (i) Counters
      (ii) Cabinet
      (iii) Sink elevators

(b) Movable equipment : Are the equipment not installed permanently with the building and which could be moved as per need :
  e.g. (i) Balances
      (ii) Desks
      (iii) Carts
      (iv) Mixtures

(c) **Personnel requirement :** A number of activities and processes are carried out in the hospital pharmacy. The activities include in manufacturing, testing, distribution, administration and procurement of materials. A team of persons with M. Pharm., B. Pharm, D. Pharm. and Microbiology qualifications will be required. The exact number of qualified persons will depend upon the size and the activity of the hospital pharmacy.

(d) **Requirement of Pharmacists :** The exact number of pharmacists required depends upon the bed size of the hospital and the nature of activities going on in the hospital pharmacy. The Medical Council of India has given minimum requirement of pharmacist, which is summarised as below :

Bed Size	Number of Pharmacists
Nil (only out-patient)	1
1 – 50	3
51 – 100	5
101 – 200	8
201 – 300	10
301 – 500	15
Above 501	15 + 1 for every 100

Chart 1 : Movement of Medicines

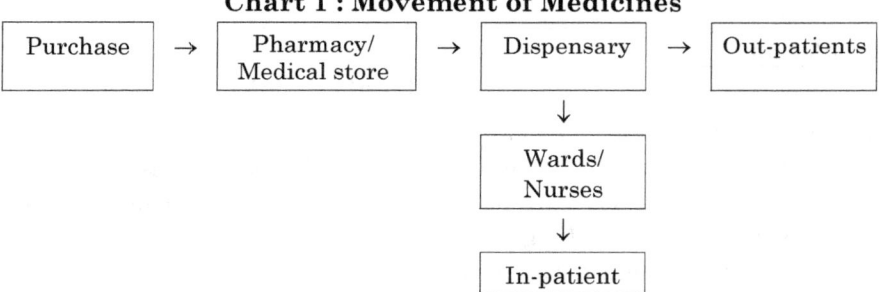

Chart 2 : Movement of Raw Material

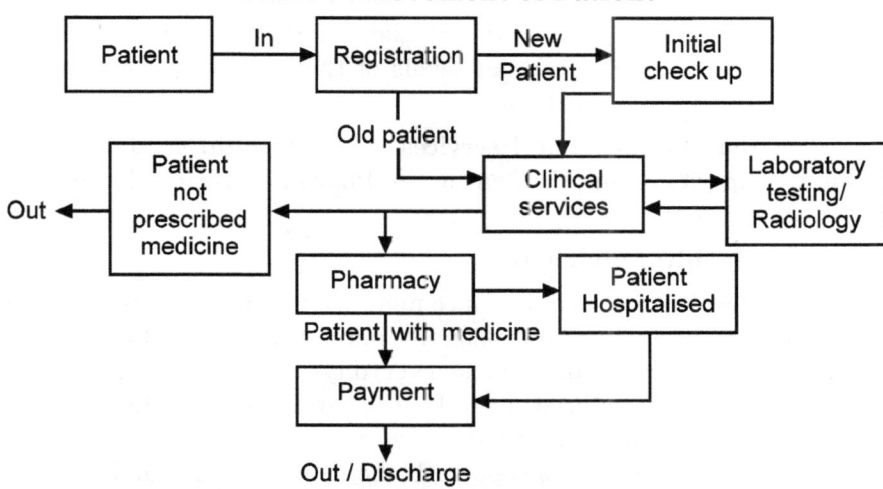

Chart 3 : Movement of Patient

ORGANISATION OF THE HOSPITAL PHARMACY

A big hospital pharmacy renders a number of services which include a number of activities; and hence has a complex organisation with integrated set-up comprising the following divisions :

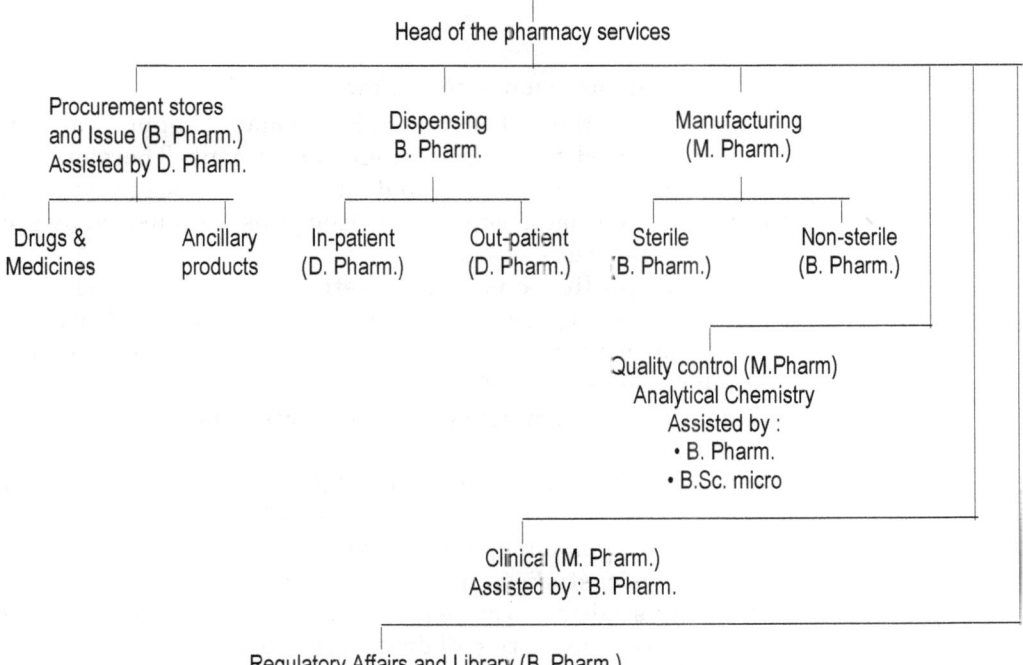

Qualifications of the Hospital Pharmacist

One should be a legally qualified (i.e. Registered Pharmacist) and professionally competent person working at different levels of the hospital pharmacy mentioned earlier in the organisational chart.

The chief of the pharmaceutical services of the hospital should be a graduate with adequate experience or M. Pharm. in Pharmaceutical science or a Ph.D. personnel is preferred.

Abilities of the Hospital pharmacist

With the modernisation and advancement in the medical field the hospital pharmacy has been providing professionally managed services to the out-patients and In-patients. Apart from this almost everyday innovations, new concepts and techniques are being introduced in different areas like technology, research, methods skills etc. The hospital pharmacist performs a vital role in all these through different activities and to cope with the needs of the time he must possess the following abilities.

The abilities are mainly categorised as :

1. Technical abilities.
2. Administrative abilities.
3. Academic abilities.

1. **Technical abilities :** These are mentioned below :
   (a) **Manufacturing knowledge :** The hospital pharmacy supplies almost all the medicines required to the In-patient department. Therefore, he must have adequate knowledge and technical background to manufacture different dosage forms. Apart from this he must be aware about the sources of the drugs, costing etc.
   (b) **Knowledge about quality control :** Testing of raw material and finished product is done by chemical, physical and analytical method with the help of the instruments like HPLC, HPTLC, autotitrator, pH meter, spectrophotometer, etc. For this purpose he must know the procedure, handling of instruments and reagents and the chemicals required for testing.
   (c) **Research ability :** He should have the ability to perform different pharmacological and toxicological, experiments pharmacokinetics and clinical trial studies on compounds under investigation.
   Apart from these basic studies, he should work on the formulation aspects like stability studies, incompatibilities – Drug to drug and drug to food interaction, sustained action of drug, formulation elegance etc.
2. **Administrative abilities :** A pharmacist should have administrative abilities because he plays a very important role in a hospital with many departments like medicine, surgery, nursing and patients for different

purpose like drug manufacturing and distribution, selection and drugs, storage and safety medicines etc. Therefore, he should know about :

(a) Material management and inventory control.

(b) Planning and Accounting.

(c) Communication skill.

(d) Patient Counselling.

(e) Knowledge about all related laws and legal regulations.

3. **Academic abilities** : For professional approach and competence in hospital pharmacy services, the Hospital Pharmacist should have the following qualities :

   (a) **Teaching quality** : He should be well-versed with the basic pharmaceutical science, sterilization, selection, storage of drugs, dispensing aspects, medication errors etc. His ability should be better than his counterparts working in different hospitals. He should develop confidence in his subordinates about his knowledge.

   (b) **Participation** : He is responsible for participation in workshops, seminars and related programmes and should be able to contribute towards educational activities of the hospital.

   (c) **Conduct of training activity** : He is also responsible for training the fellow pharmacists and nursing peoples. He should conduct educational programmes for the new staff and other professionals of the hospital.

   (d) **Retrieval of information** : He is a responsible person at Drug information centre and should have the ability to evaluate information critically. He accordingly should inform the concerned faculty of the hospital.

QUESTIONS

1. Describe the objectives of hospital pharmacy.   **[(W - 00, 01) 4 marks]**
2. Explain the functions of the hospital pharmacy.
   [(S : 97, 98 : W - 96) 4 marks]
3. Write a note on the location of the hospital pharmacy. **[(W - 00, 01) 4 marks]**
4. What are the requirements of space and equipment for the smooth working of its hospital pharmacy.   **[(W - 97) 4 marks]**
5. What are the qualifications required for a pharmacist ? What academic abilities he must develop to be successful pharmacist ?   **[(W - 97) 4 marks]**
6. Describe the abilities required by a hospital pharmacist.
   [(W - 96, 98 : S - 00) 4 marks]

■■■

3

DRUG DISTRIBUTION SYSTEM IN HOSPITALS

(The Core of Patient Care)

INTRODUCTION

The aspects of drug distribution in a hospital are distribution to the out-patient, the in-patient and the operation theatres. The procedures of drug dispensing are categorised into two groups :

(A) Ambulatory / Out-patient services.

(B) In-patient services.

(A) Ambulatory Patient Services : (Out-Patient Services)

Out patients are not occupying beds in the hospitals or clinics, but after consultation and diagnosis treatment is given without admitting to the hospital. Today hospitals are rendering out-patient services as :

(i) **Primary care :** It deals with majority care for daily personal health needs. This includes health maintenance.

(ii) **Referral or tertiary care :** This is not explanatory but it means care beyond the primary care.

(ii) **Emergency care :** These services are provided for immediate medical attention or in case of an accident.

The reasons behind the growth of the out-patient services are summarised as under :

(i) The deficiency of medical practitioners in some areas.

(ii) The need of health community.

(iii) To achieve control over patients receiving drugs after investigation.

(iv) To conduct teaching programmes as per the needs of the hospital.

Out-Patients could be categorised as follows :

1. **Emergency out-patients :** 24 hour services are given to those patients who requires immediate care for the survival.

2. **Referred out-patients :** These patients are referred to the hospital for a specific purpose due to lack of facilities available with the private clinic practitioner or the patient needs extra medical care.

3. **Special out-patient :** After completion of the general check up, the patients are asked to go for clinical, pathological or radiological examinations for accurate diagnosis. A medicine or concise of medicine is given to him after receiving the test report.

4. **General out-patient :** These patients come for check-up and medicine is prescribed to him. They may either undergo minor surgery, superficial surfing dressing at the hospital.

Location of Out-patient Dispensary :

Despite no specific rule for location, the dispensary is preferred near the main entrance of the OPD block or the location must be easily accessible to the patients.

There are three options for this :
(i) A separate out-patient pharmacy.
(ii) A combined In-patient and out-patient unit with service provided from the same window.
(iii) A combined In-patient and out-patient unit with service provided from different windows.

If a OPD is running in a individual premise or building a separate pharmacy set is required to dispense the medicines.

Layout of Dispensary :

Out-patients are the one who decide the image of the hospital as per the services received by them. So, it is essential to look into the following aspects while designing it :
(i) A separate waiting room with appropriate seating facilities.
(ii) Sufficient number of service windows and separate facility for women.
(iii) Provision for adequate light and ventilation is a must.
(iv) Civil aspects must be considered to carry out all dispensing activities.

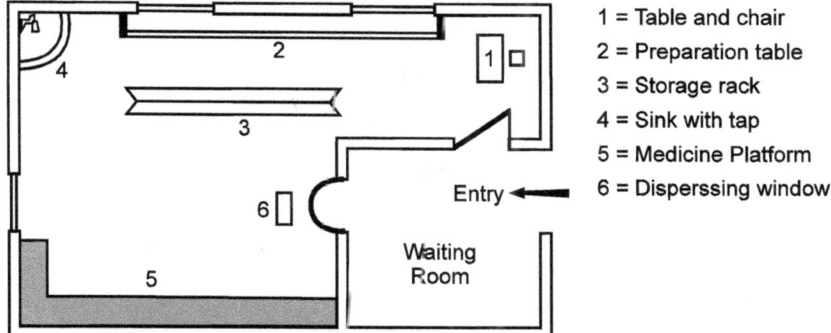

Fig. 3.1 : A Typical Plan of out-patient dispensary

Routine Dispensing to out-patient :
(i) A patient takes prescription, written by the physician, to the pharmacy, where it is dispensed by the pharmacist.
(ii) The pharmacist will ensure that the prescription in case of a waiting patient, is numerically identified and the right patient gets the right medicine.
(iii) The medicine is labelled and arranged in a container to dispense.
(iv) Appropriate instructions have been given by the pharmacist regarding dispensed medicine.
(v) Finally related records will be maintained by the pharmacist.

(B) In-Patient Services :

In-patients are those who get hospitalised for the purpose of treatment, cure of disease, surgery or rehabilitation.

Methods : In a hospital medicine is distributed to the patients by the different methods as mentioned below :

1. Individual prescription order system.
2. Complete floor stock system.
3. Combination of No. 1 and 2.
4. Unit dose dispensing.

1. Individual Prescription Order System

This system is mostly adopted in very small hospitals having a bed size of 2 to 5 and private clinics. The medicine is dispensed either by the pharmacist or under his direction. The dispensed medicine is labelled with individual patient's name with related instructions after receiving the prescription sheets from the pharmacy.

Advantages :

(i) All prescriptions are directly checked by the pharmacist.

(ii) Medication errors could be avoided.

(iii) It facilitates interaction between the pharmacist, the doctors and the nurses.

(iv) Reduced man power is required.

(v) Close control on inventory is possible.

Disadvantages :

(i) Difficulty of dispensing in absence of a pharmacist.

(ii) This system cannot be used in big hospitals.

(iii) Medicine cost may increase.

2. Complete floor stock system

Under this system both the pharmacy and the nursing station are responsible for the drug distribution. The drugs are of two categories, namely :

(a) Charge floor stock drugs

(b) Non-charge floor stock drugs.

(a) Charge floor stock drugs :

Charge floor stock drugs can be defined as those medications which are stocked at the nursing station all the times and are charged to the patient's account after their administration.

In this system the medicine is charged to the patient due to high cost, quantity used or frequency. Such medications are mainly injectables, infusions etc. The injectables generally include classes of :

(a) Antibiotics
  (i) Penicillin G potassium 20 million units
  (ii) Procaine penicillin 3 lac units/ml
  (iii) Streptomycin sulphate 1 mg/2 ml.
(b) Antiallergic
  (i) Diphenlydramine HCl 10 mg/ml
  (ii) Hydrocartisone sodium succinate 100 mg.
(c) Antihypertensive
  (i) Sorbitrate
  (ii) Reserpine HCl 0.5 mg/ml
  (iii) Atenenol
(d) Cardiovascular drugs
  (i) Depressant – procaine amide 100 mg/ml / cardiotonics
  (ii) Vasoconstrictor – phenylephrine HCl 10 mg/ml
(e) Anticoagulants
  (i) Heparin 10,000 units/ml
(f) Antiepileptic
  (i) Sodium diphenylhydantoin mg/ml.
(g) Miscellaneous
  (i) Dextrose 50%
  (ii) Manitol Inj. 25%.

Dispensing of charge floor stock drugs :

Such drugs are dispensed by :

Envelope method : A hospital develops a method in which an envelope was used to dispense the drugs to the nursing station and was also used as a charge ticket. In this system a pharmacist fills pre-labelled envelopes with the needed drugs and places a predetermined quantity on the nursing ward. At the time of administration the nurse writes the name and room number of the patient on the envelope and puts it in her "out basket". It is later sent to the pharmacy where it is priced and forwarded to the billing section of the accounting office.

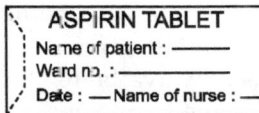

(b) Non-charge floor Stock Drugs :

These are the drugs which are kept at the nursing station for the use of all patients of the wards. In this case the cost of the medicine, is not directly added to patient's billing. The medicines cost may be calculated as per the day expenses of the hospital room.

The stock of such drugs is maintained by considering the following factors :

(i) Category of drug
(ii) Frequency of drug use
(iii) Quantity of drug needed
(iv) Cost of the drug.
(v) Inventory and budget of the hospital.

Dispensing of non-charge floor stock drugs :

To dispense this stock of medicine following methods are adopted :

1. **Drug Basket method :** This method is very commonly used in the hospitals. The night duty nurse checks the drug stock against a master list given by the pharmacy. The nurse puts a check mark on the number needed for each drug on the requisition for floor stock supplies.

   Then the duty nurse puts the empty bottles and containers alongwith requisition slip in the basket. This basket is sent to the pharmacy staff collects such drug basket and dispensed each requisition slip accordingly. And finally the basket is delivered to the floor.

2. **Mobile Dispensing unit :** It is a stainless steel specially designed cupboard or trolley with facility to carry all sizes of containers. In this system the night duty nurse need not check the drug stock. The pharmacy inspects the drug cabinet and refills empty containers. The carbon copy of the requisition for floor stock supplies is left at the nursing station as a record of delivery. By this method the pharmacist is brought out of the pharmacy and is available at the nursing wards. This increases interaction between the pharmacist and the nursing staff.

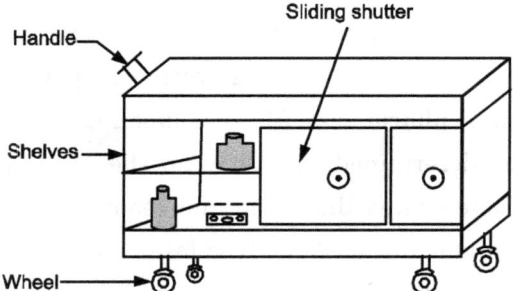

Fig. 3.2 : Mobile Dispending Unit

Advantages of complete floor stock system :

(i) Required drugs are especially available.
(ii) Minimises return of medicine to pharmacy.

(iii) Reduction in patient prescription orders.
(iv) Less number of pharmacy staff is required.

Disadvantages of complete floor stock system :
(i) Chances of increase in medication error due to reduced overview of medication order.
(ii) It increases drug inventory.
(iii) Increases hazards due to drug deterioration.
(iv) Wastage of drugs due to insufficient storage facility.

3. Combination of Method No. 1 & 2 :

This combination system is probably the most used one in hospitals. The hospitals basically follow Individual prescription order and a limited floor stock system is also employed.

4. Unit Dose Dispensing :

Unit dose medications are those which are ordered, packaged, handled, administered in single or multiple units containing predetermined amount of drug.

In this system a bulk is repacked in a single dose quantity in an individual pack. All the activities are carried out under the strict control of a pharmacist. This system could be followed by two ways :

(a) Centralised unit dose drug distribution system (CUDDS).
(b) De-centralised unit dose drug distribution system (DCUDDS).

(a) Centralised unit dose Dispensing : The total medicine is stored in the central area of the pharmacy from where it is distributed to the patients through medication carts and dumb waiters against the physicians medication order received to the pharmacy.

(b) De-centralised unit dose dispensing : This system is used in hospitals with separate buildings by following satellite pharmacies situated on each floor of the building. All activities are conducted in the satellite pharmacy and the medicine is distributed through the medication carts.

Advantages :
(i) Better stability of the product.
(ii) Duplication of order is avoided.
(iii) Avoids losses and drug wastage during handling.
(iv) Patients are charged for only those drugs which are administered.
(v) Nursing time is saved due to ready doses.
(vi) The pharmacist reviews the medication order copy and thus reduces medication error.
(vii) Contamination and other errors like labelling could be reduced.

Disadvantages :
(i) It is a time consuming activity.
(ii) The cost of the medicine may increase.

(iii) Needs more staff to prepare unit dosage.

(iv) Extra space and facilities are required.

(v) Ledger and posting becomes tedious.

Satellite Pharmacy :

The concept of satellite pharmacy is being adopted in very big hospitals which have multistoreyed separate buildings in a single premises. There, it is very difficult to cope with the distribution of drug to all the wards everyday both in the morning as well as in the evening.

So, those hospitals are running satellite pharmacies in the form of mini pharmacies, which are situated on each floor. A few days stock of medicine is stored or according to the policies of the hospitals. The main pharmacy supplies the medicines.

Advantages :

(i) Efficiently drugs can be distributed.

(ii) Time of drug distribution could be reduced.

(iii) Errors in drug distribution could be stopped.

Disadvantages :

(i) Effect on the budget of hospital.

(ii) Additional manpower is required.

Prepackaging in the hospital :

Routinely, in small and medium size hospitals, the pharmacist may prepack only those items which, he determines need to much time to dispensed. Rest of drugs are packed and dispensed as and when required in the wards and in OPD.

In European countries like U.K. the ward pharmacy being rapidly a nurturing concept, while in India it has limited extend, which begins and closes with wrapping of powders such as aspirin, boric acid etc. But many large hospitals understand, that it is an economical aspect. A large scale pre-packaging essentially needs a separate unit with separate facilities, such as equipments, storage, processing areas etc. The entire activities are to be carried out under a surveillance of pharmacist only.

It is a very difficult task, as to what and how much quantity, with what pack size to be packed ? Hence, the hospital authorities (PTC) determines same policies and facts to be considered, prior to pre-packaging. They are as :

(i) The data of utilization, for various dosage forms and therapeutic drugs.

(ii) The call-cycle of the out-patients.

(iii) Stability (Shelf-life) of the product.

(iv) Availability of the medicine in small units by the pharmaceutical manufacturer.

Advantages of Pre-packaging :
  (i) It reduces overall cost of medicine.
  (ii) It saves time of dispensing of drugs to both, out-patients and in-patients (i.e. wards).
  (iii) It ensures accuracy and accountability of dosages of drug.

Disadvantages of Pre-packaging :
  (i) Inventory.
  (ii) Required more manpower.
  (iii) Facilities : Equipment are costly.

Bed side pharmacy :

Health Authorities in countries like U.K., U.S.A. feel that it is the responsibility of the pharmacist to participate in activities going on around the patient; apart from dispensing.

In 1972 a survey was carried out by "Noel Hall" working group in U.K. and submitted a report with recommendations regarding the need of bed side services to the public health.

Medication at bed side :

Life saving drugs like neitroglycerine tablet may be kept at the bed side, if so ordered by the physician. Not more than one strip (10 tablet) shall be left with the patient. The medicine brought by the patient is not kept.

Role of Pharmacist at bed side Pharmacy :
  1. **Ward Visit :** Daily in the morning, he visits the wards and enquires about the progress of health etc.
  2. **Alloying anxiety and fright :** He shall reduce such problems by briefing the patient about the diseases, the medicine, the treatment etc.
  3. **Interaction :** He interacts with the physician about the medicines and the types of dosages forms to be prescribed. He guides to the nursing staff regarding storage, handling and safe use of the medicine.
  4. **Detailing :** He can educate the patient as well his relatives during his ward visit on epidemics, family planning communicable diseases like HIV, TB, Leprosy, AIDS and SARS etc.

Central Sterile Services : (C.S.S)

The name of the department is self-explanatory that it supplies sterile materials required in the operation theatre. Non-sterile material needed to OT is also provided.

The modern pattern of the pharmacy services incorporate C.S.S. concept which is accepted by the hospital authorities while planning with the setup of C.S.S., nursing time is saved. The related activities like sterilization, use of aseptic techniques are effectively performed.

Advantages of C.S.S. :
  (i) Reduction in ward sterilization.
  (ii) Improves general cost by reducing operational and maintenance cost.
  (iii) Nursing load is reduced, thus allowing nursing skill to wards.
  (iv) Facilitates standardization of sterilization process.

Location :

Ideally, it should be located very near to those departments, where it supplies are maximum like the operation theatre. But the central store and landing should be nearby :

Layout :

A typical plan shall allow a flow scheme of activities and working stations should be visible to the incharge. A number of working stations like Gloves processings, linen sterilization and general clean-up areas are separated from sterile storage and unsterile storage in a modern C.S.S. Due to such layout cross flow of activities and contaminated material with sterile goods is minimised. The size and types of working stations totally depend on the function of the hospital.

Typical plan : Central sterile services.

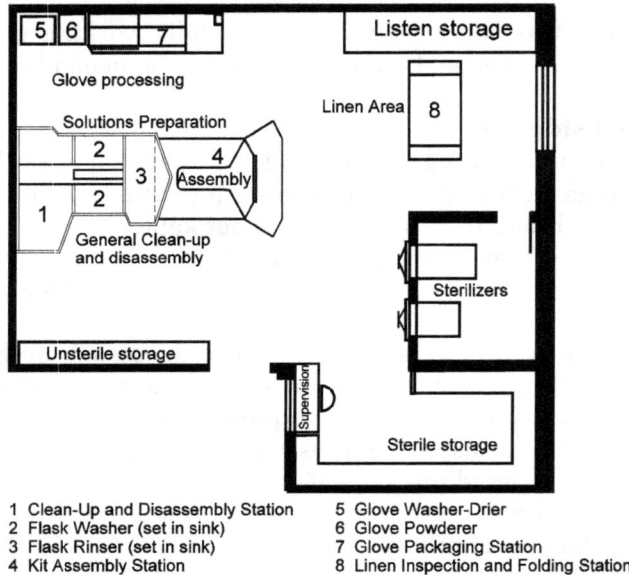

1 Clean-Up and Disassembly Station
2 Flask Washer (set in sink)
3 Flask Rinser (set in sink)
4 Kit Assembly Station
5 Glove Washer-Drier
6 Glove Powderer
7 Glove Packaging Station
8 Linen Inspection and Folding Station

Fig. 3.3

Management of staff :

A modern curriculum in pharmacy provides exposure on bacteriology, principles of sterilization, accounting and management to the students. Hence a pharmacist is an educationally better qualified person than the nurses to manage C.S.S.. The nurse has a better knowledge about the use of dispensed product. So following types of management are practised.

1. **Pharmacist controlled :**
   He is well-versed with all operations carried out in C.S.S. So he is the ideal person to head this department.
2. **Part of Nursing controlled :**
   Maximum items used are by the nurses for patient cure. Hence a senior nurse is incharge of this section.

3. **Dual controlled :**
   Both the pharmacist and the nurse do some functions like packing, distribution of medicine, supplies of O.T. requirement and cleaning etc.
   The person working in CSS should have the knowledge of the following :
   (i) Principles of sterilization.
   (ii) Methods and techniques of sterilization.
   (iii) Operation of Sterilizers like Hot air oven, autoclave.
   (iv) Details about Gaseous sterilization (Ethylene oxide)
   (v) Fundamentals of microbiology.
   (vi) Good Laboratory Practices (GLP)

Duties of Pharmacist in CSS :
The pharmacist performs the following duties in C.S.S. (Central Sterile Services).
   (i) Distribution of supplies to different departments.
   (ii) Dispensing of supplies in small lots.
   (iii) Purchase of supplies, receiving and storing.
   (iv) Interaction with sales personnel.
   (v) Meetings and Discussion on problems with medical staff.
   (vi) Teaching and lecturing to various groups.
   (vii) Implementation of standardization procedures.
   (viii) Manufacturing of bulk.
   (ix) Manufacturing of small lot of sterile and non-sterile products.

QUESTIONS

1. Who is an out-patient ? (W. 97, S. 02)
2. Explain the process of dispensing medicine to the out-patient in a hospital. (W. 00,02)
3. Write a note on the out-patient services. (W-99 : S-99)
4. How dispensing of non-floor stock drug is carried out ? (S - 96)
5. Give advantages and disadvantages of floor stock system ? (W - 01)
6. What are the advantages and disadvantages of unit dose dispensing ? (S - 96, 97, 01, 02, 04 : W - 03)
7. What do you mean by unit dose dispensing ? (W - 97 : S - 99, 01, 03)
8. Describe the different drug distribution systems in the hospital which are available for-in-patient. (S - 99, 01, 04)
9. What is bed-side pharmacy ? (W - 01, 03 : S - 02, 04)
10. Explain bed-side pharmacy. (W - 00 : S - 96, 97)
11. Write note on bed side pharmacy. (S - 99)
12. Give various administrative partners of CSS. (S - 97)
13. What are the duties of pharmacist in CSS ? (W - 03)
14. Write note in C.S.S. (W- 03)

■■■

4

PROCUREMENT OF STORES AND INVENTORY CONTROL

(The Soul of Formulation)

INTRODUCTION

An inventory control can be explained as the sum of value of raw materials, fuels, spare parts, maintenance of consumable, semi-processed and finished goods stock of an organisation at any given time of point.

The hospital authorities/management should constantly monitor the requirements for inventory against the preference of liquidity. If the hospital pharmacy has too little inventory it will affect the manufacturing efficiency, and will result out of stock for supply to the in-patients as well as the out-patients high inventory will affect the overall budget of a hospital, therefore, inventory level shall be optimum.

Advantages of Inventory Control :
- Helps in maintaining inventories as less as possible with respect of drug distribution.
- It reduces chances of "out of stock" danger.
- Market and economic conditions about availability of drugs could be forecast.
- Proper records could be maintained to report to the authorities.

A number of techniques are used to control the inventory. The commonly used are :
- ABC Analysis
- VED Analysis
- FSN Analysis
- Economic Order Quantity.

ABC Analysis :

ABC means "Always Better Control". In a to big hospital pharmacy, large inventory items are stocked. These materials are grouped in three categories given in the following table as A, B and C.

'A' Category	'B' Category	'C' Category
Costly items come under this category. The volume of material may not be more than 10% of the total items but consumes 70% of the total budget of inventories.	These items are neither costly nor cheap. Items coming under this category comprise 20% of the total quantity and 20% of the expenditure from total quantity and inventory respectively.	This category items are cheaper, they contribute to 70% of items of total quantity and 10% investment of the total inventory.

(4.1)

- **VED Analysis :**
  VED analysis means,
  $$V = \text{Vital}$$
  $$E = \text{Essential}$$
  $$D = \text{Desirable}$$
  This technique is mainly adopted for control of spare parts divided in the above three groups as vital items, essential items and desirable items. The stock of spare parts is maintained by keeping in mind the criticality of production.
- **FSN Analysis :** FSN Analysis means fast, slow and non-moving items analysis. It suppose to be established by an individual organisation at its own by analysing the gravity of consumption of a material or item e.g. a pharma company can be categories :
  * Fast moving : Antibiotics
  * Slow moving : Antimalerials
  * Non-moving : Tonics and Topicals

  Because,

  Antibiotics - Require throughout the year

  Antimalerial - Generally seasonal requirement

  Tonics - Really prescribed.
- **Economic Order Quantity (EOQ) :**
  This technique is used to find out, how much quantity of medicine is to be ordered. The accurate quantity to purchase is the quantity at which the ordering cost and inventory carrying cost will be minimum.

  Ordering cost consists of cost of paper and works involved in placing the order (Paper, typing, postage etc.).

  Inventory cost comprises   — Rent of storage

                                    — Taxes

                                    — Salaries of store personnels

                                    — Losses (handling, breakage)

There are three methods which are used to determine the economic order quantity :

(i)   Tabular determination

(ii)   Graphic presentation

(iii)   Algebric formulae.

Algebric formulae method is very commonly used to place an order in units.

$$EOQ = \sqrt{\frac{2ab}{CS}}$$

where,   a = annual consumption

                 b = buying cost

                 C = cost/unit

                 S = inventory carrying cost

For example :

Annual consumption of paracetamol tablets are 1,00,000 units. The ordering cost is Rs. 7.00 and unit cost Rs. 0.75/- with inventory carrying cost of 24%.

So,
$$EOQ = \sqrt{\frac{2ab}{CS}}$$
$$= \sqrt{\frac{2 \times 1,00,000 \times 7}{0.75 \times 0.24}}$$
$$= 2789 \text{ units}$$

Procurement and Stores :

Purchasing is a function of procuring materials, storage of supplies and services required for the manufacture of a product.

Scientific purchasing is the buying of raw materials of the right quality, in the right quantities at the right time and the right price from the right source. These are the 5 "R"s of purchasing.

Objectives of Scientific Purchasing :

(i) To procure at a competitive rate.

(ii) To ensure the best quality of product.

(iii) To develop a faith and goodwill of hospital.

Procurement Procedure : The procurement involves different steps and is headed by the purchase head, who issues the purchase order :

(i) **Purchase indent :** It is also called purchase requisition. It is a formal request made to the purchase department to purchase the required materials. Generally, the indents are prepared in triplicate by all identing departments. The original copy is sent to the purchase department, the IInd copy to the store and the IIIrd copy remains with the originating department.

(ii) **Scrutinising the purchase indent :** A purchase indent describes the items either by brand names, chemical names, specifications for quality and quantity to be procured. So, indent must be scrutinised for accuracy and completeness of description.

(iii) **Market survey and selection of vendor :** An indent is a step of market survey and selection of sources of supply. In this, the items are segregated into groups, information is reversals asking of quotation to select the proper vendor who can supply

...... the right quality

...... at the right price

...... buyers quantity requirements

(iv) Order preparation : A purchase order is a legal document and serves as an evidence of agreement between the buyer and the supplier (vendor). The order form consists of the detailed description of each and every item being purchased.

Seven copies are prepared and sent to the different departments with the specific purpose :

I^{st} copy : Sent to the vendor for supply of materials.

IInd copy : Retained by the purchase officer for filling.

IIIrd copy : Sent to account department for audit.

IVth copy : Sent to finance department to release the payment to the party.

V^{th} copy : To the excise division for their reference.

VIth copy : Sent to the store, where the material will be receipt, received as information.

VIIth copy : Sent to the department, from where the indent originate.

Purchase Requisition : Hospital purchases are of a specific quality, because these materials are required to produce "Life-saving" medicine. In patho-clinical labs, blood banks and Radiology examination and for the diagnosis of the disease too. So, the specifications for the pharmacy purchases are drawn, and then purchase requisition is prepared. It consists of particulars of the item, its price and quantity alongwith the balance stock and the future requirement. The original copy is sent to the purchase officer after approval by the administrative head.

		Department of Pharmacy ABC Hospital - Mumbai PURCHASE REQUISITION				
To :		Order No. :			Enquiry No. : Date :	
SN	Code No.	Particulars	Unit	Unit cost	Quantity	Remark
Prepared by : _____				Approved by : _____		

Types of purchases : There are four methods used to purchase the materials :

1. **Centralised purchases :** Specifications for hospital purchases are drawn for the entire hospital. They are done by a purchase committee or a purchase incharge.

2. **Decentralised purchases :** The purchases are done departmentwise by its head. In a hospital pharmacy the medical officer or the head of pharmacy has the authority to purchase medicine from different sources like :
   (i) The local market - In case of emergency.
   (ii) By inviting bids - For institutional supply.
   (iii) Direct purchase - From the vendor or the manufacturer.
3. **Rate contract :** Rate contract is type of purchase, where a yearly agreement signed between the hospital authorities and supplier in which a rate for all the supplies remains constant through out the year on which they agreed upon.
4. **The tender system of hospital purchasing :**
   (i) **Open tender :** This system is mainly practised or suitable to large hospitals, controlled under Central Government, State Government and Trust. The entire procedure of tender system, is under the control of the administrator of the hospital. Tender is a written offer to supply the goods or perform a specific job a site. The system includes the following steps :
      1. **Inviting of tenders :** The tenders are invited by publishing the advertisement either in newspapers or by other means, specifying all the details regarding the quality, quantity etc. of the material being procured from several suppliers.
      2. **Scrutiny of tenders :** After receiving the tenders within the time schedule, they are scrutinised with respect of technical and economical aspect. This exercise is carried out by the formally framed committee, which works under the surveillance of administrator of hospital.
      3. **Inviting the supplier :** Then the above activity is succeeded into inviting the supplier, who complies the technical and economical standards of the tender.

      Lastly a formal agreement (i.e. purchase order) is prepared to execute the order.
   (ii) **Limited tender :** This method is suitable for private hospitals or pharmaceutical companies, in which the known suppliers are asked to furnish the details in accordance to the need and then a single supplier is offer a tender to supply the material, after scrutiny.
   (iii) **Single tender :** In case of urgency or a single item is to be procured, only a single supplier directly offer to supply the material, this is called a single tender.
   (iv) **Global tender :** When imported material, equipment or machinery are to be procured, the tenders are invited around globe; the country which supplies.

Testing of Raw Material :

On receipt of the raw material, the details of supply are entered in a entry register and a control reference code/number is allotted to each items. Intimation is given to Q.C. department. The Q.C. chemist samples the materials receipt by the store till then the material is kept in a separate area, namely "under test". On approval of the material if it complies the test then it is shifted to the main store and it is labelled as "Approved". If it does not comply with the test, it is labelled as "Rejected" and sent back to the supplier.

The approved materials are issued to the production department against their requisition. While issuing the materials FIFO (First In First Out) method is adopted. Bin Cards are tagged to each material.

The Quality Control Department performs the following tests :
1. Physical test on packing material.
2. Chemical testing
3. Instrumental Analysis
   (a) Small instruments
   (b) Sophisticated instrument
4. Microbiology testing
   (a) Sterility
   (b) Pyrogen
   (c) LAL (Limulus Amebocyte Lysate)
5. Acute toxicity :
   (a) LD – 50
   (b) Histamine reactions.

QUESTIONS

1. Write a note on Inventory Control in hospital pharmacy. **[(S - 03) 4 marks]**
2. What is Economic Order Quantity ? **[(S - 96, 00) 4 marks]**
3. How are the materials procured in a hospital ? **[(W - 03, S - 99) 4 marks]**
4. What do you mean by centralised or decentralised purchases ?
   [(W - 02, 01, 00, 97) 4 marks]
5. Describe the methods of procurement in a hospital ? **(W - 99)**
6. What is the purchase requisition ? To whom it is sent for procurement ?
   [(S - 02, 97 : W - 00) 4 marks]
7. How is the testing of pharmaceutical raw materials conducted in a hospital ?
   [(S - 99) 4 marks]

■■■

5
HOSPITAL MANUFACTURING
(The Spirit of Production)

INTRODUCTION

In India hospital manufacturing is one of the greatest challenges for the hospital authorities. Besides this, the issue was referred for the study to the "Hathi Committee". It studied it in accordance to feasibility, *financial* implications, utilisation of available resources and per day requirement of medicines. Apart from this, the Committee recommended the following criteria, why the hospital/Institute should have its own manufacturing facility.

1. **Quality of medicine :** To some extent unfair practice by the supplier leads to supply of sub-standard medicine.
2. **Unavailability of drugs :** Certain drugs either due to the less margin of profit or an quantity of the order is less, remain out of stock in the market.
3. **Delay in supply :** Purchases from outside the institute require sometime to complete the procurement formalities. It may lead to delay in supply.
4. **Cost :** It is the most important factor. If the daily requirement of medicine is in large quantities, which is above the break-even point. It is a point at which no profit or loss occurs.

Economic Considerations

Prime activity of the hospital pharmacy is to ensure supply of medicine to a patient either by manufacturing in the pharmacy itself or by purchasing from outside pharmaceutical companies through institutional supply.

Similarly, the "Mysore Committee" on hospital pharmacies, suggested to have own I.V. fluid manufacturing facility. From an economical point of view, need of infrastructure, machinery, manpower, compliance with standards of FDA and working capital is essential to run a manufacturing unit. The entire operation affects the budgetary control of the hospital. Therefore, it is beyond the scope of the hospital authorities to install the I.V. fluid manufacturing facility.

Estimation of Demand :

Prior to manufacturing any product, the manufacturer should have the list of types and quantity of medicine/drugs to be produced. A hospital shall arrive at the requirement and future demands by "forecasting".

Estimation of the demand can be determined by the different methods, such as :

1. **Reference of past history :** The data of medicines consumed by the pharmacy are extended to the future, in deciding the demand of drugs.
2. **Judgemental :** The opinion of clinical and pharmacy staff of a hospital is taken into consideration regarding the requirements of medicine in the future.
3. **Casual models :** By evaluating the medical documents of patients in a hospital, one can forecast the demands for a specific category of drug depends on certain facts.

S. No.	Category of drug	Facts
1.	Whole blood	Number of casualty admitted in emergency wards.
2.	Anti-hypertensive	Number of patients admitted every month with hypertension.
3.	Radio-pharmaceuticals	Number of patients came for screening (diagnostic examination) periodically.

Unit Cost :

The total cost per unit is calculated by assuming that the land and premises are own and no rent is paid on account of it. It is calculated by using a formula :

$$\text{Cost per unit} = \frac{\text{Total cost}}{\text{Total Number of Units packed}}$$

The total cost of the product is determined as :

$$\text{Total cost} = \text{Variable cost} + \text{Fixed cost}$$

where,

Variable cost includes :
- Cost of Raw materials
- Cost of Packaging materials
- Utility expenses
- Wages

Fixed cost includes :
- Salaries
- Marketing expenses
- Administrative expenses
- Testing charges (Q.C.)
- Depreciation value of machine and premises.

Sterile Manufacturing :

In 1616, the discovery of blood circulation by Harvey gave a base to formulate parenterals in the form of injectables and intravenous admixtures and fluids. The word parenterals is derived from a Greek word.

Para = Beside

Enteron = Gastrointestinal tract

Mainly parenterals are classified into two groups as LVP (Large Volume Parenterals) and SVP (Small Volume Parenterals) which could be differentiated as under :

Sr. No.	Criteria	LVP	SVP
1.	Pack size	100 ml and more	1 to 99 ml.
2.	Type of containers used for packing	Generally plastic bottles	Glass/Umble colour ampoules and Vials.
3.	Vehicles used	Water for Injection	WFI or oils like PG - 400 and PG - 600.
4.	Added substances	No added substance	Preservatives, anti-oxidants and microbials are added.
5.	Sterilization	Terminal sterilization	Generally aseptic fill products.
6.	Administered	With I.V. set	With syringes and needles.
7.	Uses	Clinically as supportive measure or nutrient	Diagnostic or Therapeutic purpose.

PG = Propylene Glycols.

Containers And Closures :

The material used for packaging of parenteral product should be of a very high quality, which must comprise the qualities as below :

1. Must be physically and chemically inert.
2. Must be adequately transparent to observe the product.
3. Do not permit diffusion across either side.
4. Must have adequate strength for holding the product during shipment.

Glass containers : Glass is used as the container material of choice for most injectables. It is composed of silicon dioxide with percentage of other oxides such as sodium, calcium, potassium, magnesium, iron and boron. The basic structure of glass is formed by silicon oxide and boric oxide.

The borosilicate glass material is classified as under :

1. **Type I, Borosilicate :** Mainly it is composed of silicon dioxide and boric oxide, because such composition offers high resistance to alkali attack.

2. **Type II, Borosilicate :** It comprises of compounds of relatively high percentage of sodium and calcium oxides. This makes the glass chemically less resistant and offers alkali attack, because of the surface treatment with sulphur dioxide.

3. **Type III, Borosilicate :** It is a soda lime glass which offers moderate alkali attack and not used as a container for parenterals; but used for oral liquids or dry syrups.

4. **N.P. Glass :** It is exclusively composed of soda lime or soda ash which is not suitable for containers used for parenteral preparations.

Hydrolytic Resistance Test :

The test is performed on glass containers, which will be used for packing according to the pharmacopoeia.

Principle : It is based on blank determination of acid-base titration. In this the alkali released into a solution during thermal sterilization, is titrated with 0.01 M HCl using methyl red as an indicator, giving a colour change from yellow to pink.

Plastics : Plastics can be defined as substances which can be easily moulded by application of heat and pressure.

Plastics are broadly divided into two groups :

1. **Thermostat :** This is the plastic that cannot be recycled once it is fabricated e.g. Bakelite.

2. **Thermoplastics :** These can be recycled e.g.

    e.g. PVC – Polyvinyl chloride

    PP – Poly propylene

    PE – Poly ethylene

Chemically plastics are organic compounds. They are made by polymerisation of number of small molecules called monomers. "Parenterals" can be packed in containers made from thermoplastics.

Ideal requirements :

- Must be an inert one and non-toxic.
- No additive from the plastic material should migrate.
- There should be least permeability of water vapour / gases as possible.
- No surface adsorption of drug from the solution.

Differentiation between glass and plastic containers :

Sr. No.	Criteria	Glass containers	Plastic containers
1.	Weight	High weight materials	Light weight materials.
2.	Nature	Brittle ones	Non-brittle, but collapsible.
3.	Chemical compatibility.	Release alkali into solution on thermal sterilization.	Inert one with solution on heating.
4.	Transparency	Transparent	Less transparent or slightly opaque.
5.	Shipment	Shipment needs handling with special care.	Shipment becomes convenient.
6.	Packing and closure sealing.	With the aid of machine.	FFS (Form, Fill and Seal) technology.

ASEPTIC AREA

It is essential to have a clean area (Aseptic area) for the manufacturing of Parenteral formulations, because of their direct administration into the blood circulation. It is an entirely sealed area from outside *atmosphere* to keep aseptic environment free from *physical* and *biological* contaminations.

Therefore, at the time of designing and constructing the aspectic area one must keep in mind the essentials, which composes of civil work to HVAC (High Ventilating and Air conditioning) system including the electrical wire fittings and switches.

The walls facing outside should have double walled glass partition. The material used should protect the wall, flooring and ceiling from material handling, routine CIP and SIP of equipments and chemicals which are used for fumigation of aseptic area extruded Plastic, Aluminium, Terazzo and Epoxy paints should be used. Coving need to be done to all the corners formed between wall to wall, wall to floor and ceiling to prevent accumulation of micro-organisms.

The personnels working in such areas must follows the guidelines and standards of behaviour in aspectic area according to GMP.

Aseptic area can be classified on the basis of nature of environment.

- **Class 100 :** Area where number of particles of size > 0.5 micron per cubic feet of air should not be more than 100.
- **Class 10,000 :** Number of particles per cubic feet of air of a size > 0.5 micron and > 5.0 micron should not be more than 10,000 and 70 respectively.
- **Class 100,000 :** Number of particles per cubic feet of air of a size > 0.5 micron and 5.0 micron should not be greater than 100,000 and 700 respectively.

To achieve and maintain the above standards of aseptic environment, the following things are essential.
- Positive pressure.
- Cool air (25 – 27°C) and Relative humidity.
- HEPA and Laminar flow.
- U.V. Light lamps.

General requirements :
- Sterile garments.
- Gum boots.
- Surgical gloves.
- Disinfectant solution.

HEPA : HEPA means High Efficient Particulate Air. HEPA filters are of different sizes fitted into the ceiling of aseptic area and "Laminar air flow" bench. The air flow should either horizontal or vertical in parallel direction with a velocity of 100 ± 20 ft. per min. And the air size of 0.3 micron is filtered at a rate of 99.97% efficiency.

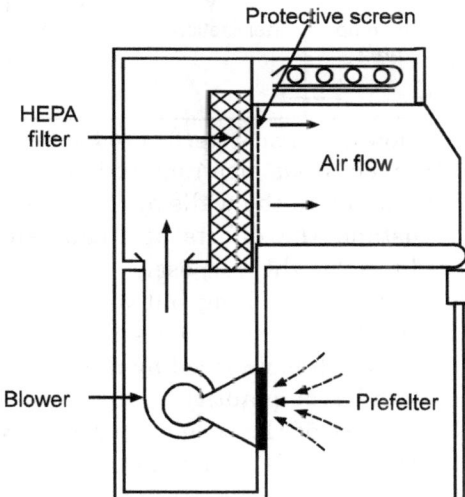

Fig. 5.1 : Laminar flow air bench

Laminar air flow bench is used to perform sterility and other micro-biological testing like bio-assay. There are two types :
- Vertical
- Horizontal

Air being a major source of contamination, should be passed through a glass wool prefilter of 5.0 micron size, via blower. The electrostat and dehumidifiers control the air born particles and percentage humidity by precipitating the particles due to opposite electrical charges. Electrical heaters reduce the moisture content of air respectively.

Applications :
(i) In pharma (parenterals) company.
(ii) In micro-biological areas.
(iii) In electronics and computer technology industries.
(iv) In airplanes and fighter planes.
(v) In operation theatre.

Sterile Production Facility

The product being produced runs through different areas in sequence before it is finished and packed. So such areas should be well-connected with each other and should be free from physical and biological contaminations. These areas are subdivided as :

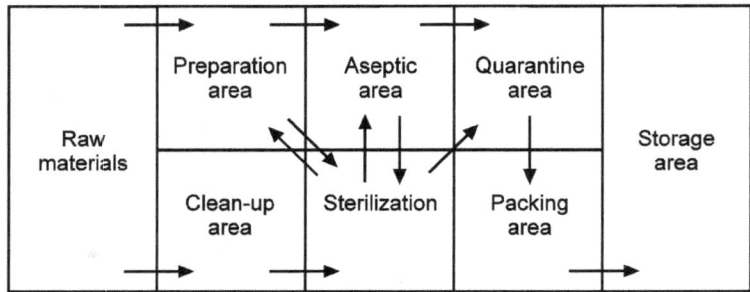

Fig. 5.2 : Flow diagram of sterile production facility

1. **Clean-up area :** In such areas cleaning and steaming of packing materials and utensils is done; therefore the walls and ceiling are constructed in such a way, that they withstand the effects of steam and chemicals. Generally, epoxy paint is coated to solve the purpose.

2. **Compounding area :** It is nothing but a "preparation" area, where the formula is compounded; and not necessarily aseptic. The entire day's required raw material which is received by the store and is used according to the type of product with batch quantity.

3. **Aseptic area :** It is heart of the whole operation where fabrication, filling and sealing of product is done. It is divided into sub-sections such as :
   (a) Entry section
   (b) Fabrication section.

   (a) Entry section : It comprises three different rooms with different objectives.
   * **Air Lock :** Air lock is an entry section of aseptic area comprising increase of air velocity in order to air lock I, II and III.
   * **Air Lock I :** Here facilities to wash hands and feet and to keep the aprons and caps are provided.
   * **Air Lock II :** It is also called the gowning room when street cloths are replaced by sterile garments and gum boots.
   * **Air Lock III :** It is a walking room to enter the main area. Here antiseptic solution is kept in dispensers to mop the surgical gloves.

Requirements of Aseptic area (Clean up area)

(i) Laminar flow with a velocity of 90 ± 20 ft./min.

(ii) Positive pressure.

(iii) Air changes (sterile corr. 20/min, mixing room 20/min and 40/min in filling room)

(iv) Temp. 20 – 25°C with a humidity of 50 - 60% RH.

(v) U.V. lamps.

(vi) Disinfection of miscellaneous items.

(vii) Periodical fumigation/Disinfection of area.

(viii) Sterile garments like :

* Gown
* head gear of mask
* gum boots etc.

Maintenance and Monitoring of Aseptic area (precautions) :

Maintaining the clean and sanitized conditions of aseptic area requires careful working precautions by the expertly trained personnel. A planned schedule of cleaning is to be developed, ranging from daily to weekly or monthly, in accordance of the location and its relation to the most critical class 100 area. For this sanitization, disinfection and personnel hygiene are most significant.

Sanitization : Since, it is not possible to sterilize every item/equipment or material going to aseptic (clean) room area, it becomes more important to control the area of aseptic room by undertaking the process of proper sanitization. Sanitization of only machine surfaces is not enough, but that of the surfaces (walls, floors, ceilings, etc.) of the aseptic room is also of equal importance.

The sanitization includes general cleaning and disinfection, but the major difference in this case is the dry cleaning with a dry type vacuum cleaner, which is not involved in disinfection process.

Disinfection : Chemicals which destroy micro-organism, but not usually spores are known as disinfectants. They do not necessarily kill all micro-organisms, but reduce them to an acceptable level.

One of the important criteria required is that disinfection can take place only when the surface to be disinfected is clean and free from detergent. Residue of soil or detergents can reduce the effectiveness of the disinfectant.

Personnel hygiene : Human being contribute markedly to products contamination by releasing non-viable (inert) and viable (micro-organisms) material in a continuous shower of material. The contamination mainly results from :

- Shading of skin flakes and scales.
- Fragments of human hair.
- Droplets of moisture from coughing and breathing.
- Cosmetics etc.
- Lint fibers and starch particles from washable fabrics.

A absolute growing and strictly follow-up of cGMP guidelines for behaviour in aseptic room area is must.

The following table showing some activities contributing to particulate contamination in aseptic (clean) room area :

Activity	No. of Particles generated
Heavy activity	15,000 / min.
Moderate activity	8,000 / min.
Slight activity	4,000 / min.
Sneezing	10,00,000 / sneeze

The check points for monitoring of aseptic area mainly includes :

Physical control : It includes monitoring of non-viable air born particles, which are mainly generated by the dynamic movement of machines and personnel working in aseptic room area. A automatically operated air borne particle counter equipment is used to check the number of particles present per cu. ft. in aseptic room area. Then accordingly cleaning is done if necessary.

Biological control : Bio-burden (micro-organism) is to examine in the aseptic room area, whether micro-organisms are in the limit or not, by performing the following tests :

(i) Air sampling (culture media strip) method.

(ii) Plate count method.

Personnel control : It is already explained above that the human being is the major source of contamination, who neither be sterilized nor disinfected.

Hence, only restricted number of personnel are allowed to work in clean room area, who generally faced medical check to examine the disease status by performing the following test :

Swab test : A swab of cotton wool is placed in mouth (oral cavity) for few minutes. Then that swab is innoculated on a suitable media such as thioglycolate or casein digest. Then incubated at specified temperature and time (days). Lastly the growth of micro-organism is their or not is examined. The person found to be infectious will not be allowed to enter the aseptic room area.

Disinfection of Aseptic area :

Disinfection can be done by two ways as mentioned below :

1. **By using aerosol disinfector :** e.g. Otisafe and Oticare etc.
2. **By fumigation method :** e.g. formalin solution, isopropyl alcohol etc.

Aerosol types of disinfectors are available in different capacity (sizes), depending on their utility. Generally, they are in portable sizes with weights ranging from 5 to 7 kg. The speed of automizing lies between 45 - 60 ml/min. A desired concentration of formalin or isopropyl alcohol with water is used to produce aerosol along with water vapour. These penetrate into very fine cracks, joints of coving, crevice etc. including miscellaneous furniture or equipment which lie in the aseptic area or the operation theatre.

Following solutions, used in different dilution, are summarised in the following table.

Sr. No.	Material	Strength (%)	Quantity of Disinfectant	WFI
1.	Phenol	1.0	1000 ml	q.s. 10 lit.
2.	BKC (50%)	0.2	400 ml	q.s. 10 lit.
3.	IPA	70	7.0 ml	q.s. 10 lit.
4.	Aldekol - H	2.5	250 ml	q.s. 10 lit.

2. Fumigation :

To maintain clean room standards, periodical fumigation of the aseptic area is necessary. It is the process to make the environment free from microbes by fumes of formalin. Formalin is a potent disinfectant in vapour form which, can penetrate small crevices and fine cracks also. It is widely accepted for fumigation of clean area.

Method :

(i) The room or the O.T. should be cleaned and disinfected by using a suitable disinfectant solution explained in above table.

(ii) With the help of the adhesive tape, all cracks, crevices and openings etc. should be sealed off, leaving only the exit door.

(iii) Take the formalin solution in S.S. container after calculating the quantity which depends on the area of room and frequency of fumigation (5 ml'/m^3) with WFI.

(iv) Place the S.S. container on hot plate and switch it "on".

(v) Then seal the exit door from outside and allow the area or the O.T. to fumigate overnight.

(vi) Next day morning remove the seal in exactly the reverse manner and switch off the hot plate.

(vii) Eliminate the fumes of formalin by exhaust system.

(viii) Before using the area take the bacterial count.

(b) Fabrication section :

Mixing of ingredients in mixing tanks, filtration of bulk, filling of bulk into container and finally sealing or closures and cap are carried out under strictly aseptic conditions.

Qualities required of water for injection :

Water for injection has the greatest importance as a vehicle for the parenteral preparations. A vehicle normally has no therapeutic activity and is non-toxic. Water of suitable quality for compounding and rinsing product surfaces may be prepared either by distillation or by reverse osmosis, to meet required qualities of water for injection. Hence, the following tests performed accordingly from various official books are summarized as :

(i)	Appearance	Clear, colourless liquid.
(ii)	pH	Between 5 and 7 (Alternatively pH may be examine by acidity or alkalinity test by using indicators such as - methyl red and bromothymol blue respectively.
(iii)	Test for Ammonium	Solution shall not produces more intense colour as per I.P. - 96.
(iv)	Test for calcium and magnesium	A pure blue colour shall be obtained as per I.P. 96.
(v)	Heavy metals	Not more than 0.1 PPM by 'D' method of I.P. 96.
(vi)	Nitrates	A colour of test solution shall be less intense that standard solution as per I.P. 96.
(vii)	Sulphates	It must comply the I.P. 96 standard.
(viii)	Chlorides	It must comply the I.P. 96 standard.
(ix)	Oxidisable matters	A solution remains faint pink as per I.P. 96 test.
(x)	Residue on evaporation	Not more than 0.001% as per I.P. 96.
(xi)	Pyrogen test	Rabbit test as per I.P. 96. Dose : 10 ml/kg body weight of animal.
(xii)	Toxicity test	As per I.P. 96. Dose : 0.5 ml/mice should be non-toxic as per I.P.
(xiii)	Sterility	It should be sterile as per I.P.

Process of Sterile Manufacturing (Fabrication)

For SVP : A number of steps are involved in fabrication of formulation which start from "P" and ends with "P", which means **Preparation** of containers and **Packing** of product containers.

(i) **Preparation of containers :** The containers (vials or ampoules) are subjected to washing and cleaning after unpacking from supply boxes with D. water. Dry heat method is employed for sterilisation.

(ii) **Preparation of closures for vials :** Closures are basically prepared from rubber which need assurance for compatibility. They involve :

* Treatment with soap solution.
* Washing, cleaning and rinsing with distilled water to remove traces of detergent and fibres.
* Soaking with same additives being used in formulation for 24 hrs. or autoclaving with same.
* Rinsing and drying is done.

(iii) **Formulation :** It consists of number of the following, activities :

* Weighing of R.M. as per batch card.
* Dissolving ingredients in sequence in the vehicle.
* Adjustment of volume and pH. Then filtration of bulk.
* Filling of bulk in containers. (Aseptic)
* Sealing or capping of containers.
* Sterilization of product (if terminally sterilize).

(iv) **Packing :** It includes :

* Visual inspection
* Labelling
* Cartoning, boxing and packing of boxes.

(v) **Sampling and testing :** A number of tests are conducted on the final packed product as per the official pharmacopoeia. These tests ensures the release of the product :

* physical
* chemical
* microbiological.

Different Additives used for parenterals (SVP) :

Sr. No.	Additive	Significance	Examples
1.	Vehicles	* To dissolve water soluble solutes. * To dissolve water insoluble substances.	* Water for injection sterile WFI. * Penut oil, glycerine propylene glycol etc.
2.	Buffers	To maintain the pH of product.	* Phosphate * Acetate * Pthalate etc.
3.	Antimicrobials preservatives	* Prevent growth of micro-organisms.	* Benzyl alcohol * Benzalkonium chloride * Cresol etc.
4.	Anti-oxidants	* Prevent the oxidative degradation of product.	* Sodium sulphite * Sodium metabisulphite * Ascorbic acid etc.
5.	Stabilizers	* Ensure the stability of drug.	* EDTA
6.	Tonicity contributor	* To be isotonic with blood serum.	* Sodium chloride * Dextrose etc.
7.	Wetting and suspending agent	* To maintain formulation aspects like sedimentation, defloculation and emulsification.	* Acacia * Methyl cellulose * Gelatin * Tregacant etc.

A Typical Floor Plan – Glass Line for SVP/LVP

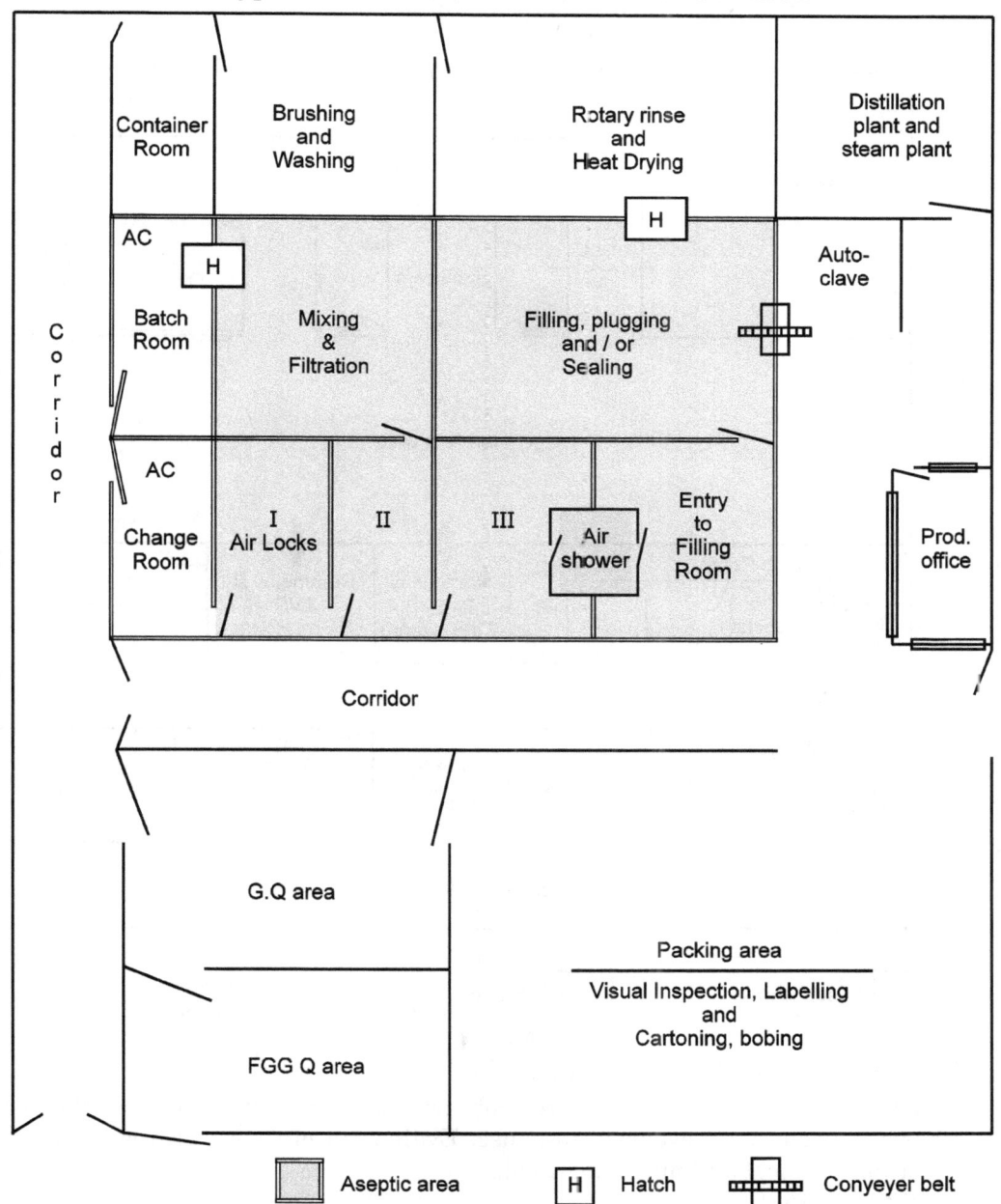

Fig. 5.3

A Typical Floor Plan – of SVP/LVP : Plastic Line

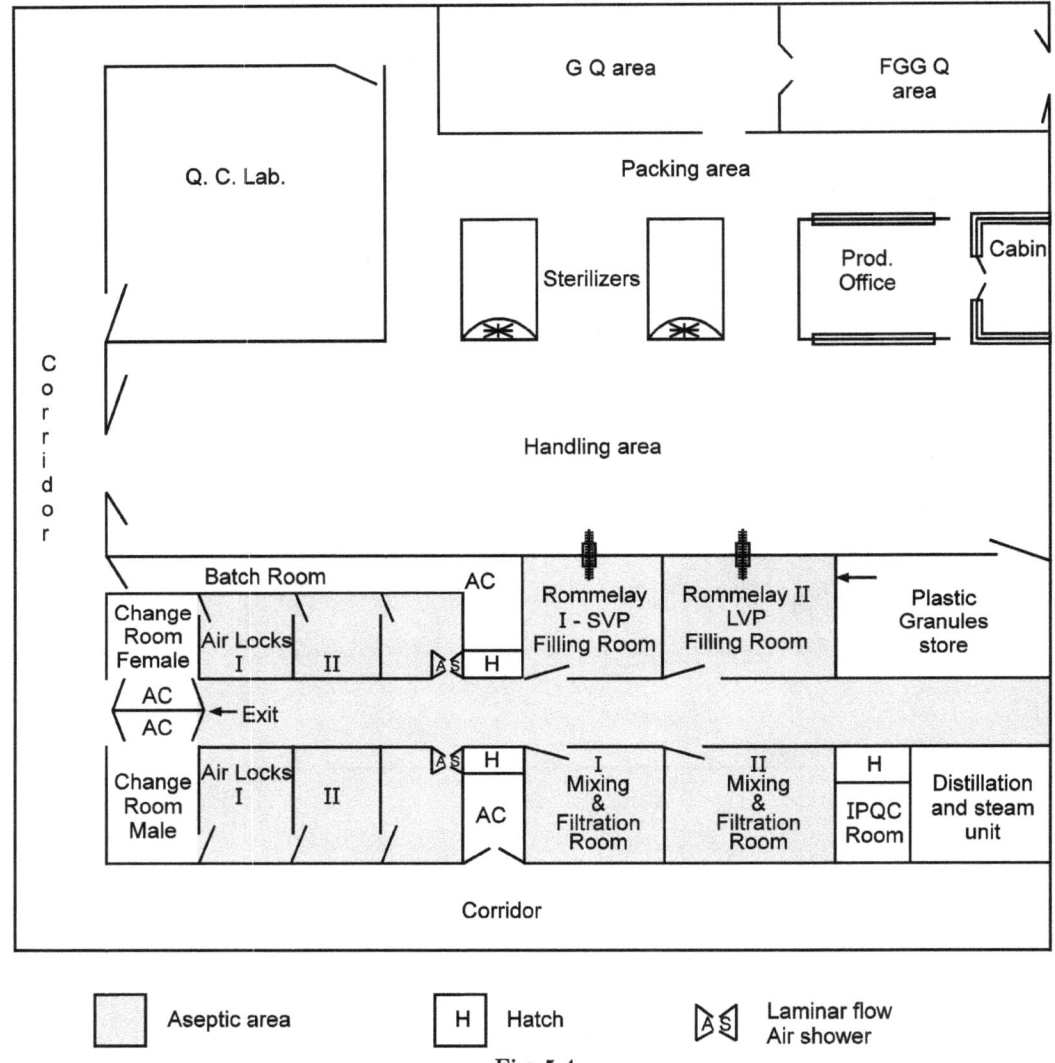

Fig. 5.4

Finished Product Evaluation tests :

Numerous tests listed into "test protocol" are performed which may be official as per pharmacopoeia and developed in-house. Evaluation is done in three categories i.e. physical, chemical and microbiological.

PHYSICAL TESTS

- **Leak test :** The entire ampoules are kept in a vacuum pump unit under negative pressure. Leaked ampoules content oozes out, then the ampoules are submerged in the dye solution of 1% methylene blue completely. The Dye solution enters the leaked ampoule, which turns the colour of the product blue. Such ampoules are rejected from the batch.

- **Clarity test :** Particulate matter in the solution consists of mobile, randomly scattered substances, other than gas bubbles. Injectable solutions should essentially be free from visible particulate matter.

The containers are exposed to white and black media under adequate light to see black and white particles respectively.

CHEMICAL TESTS

Important tests like pH, assay, limit test and oxidising matters are conducted as per their monograph in pharmacopoeia.

MICROBIOLOGICAL

Injectables, directly administered into the body, must qualify SAL (sterility assurance level). Hence to ensure SAL, especially sterility and pyrogen tests are performed.

- **Sterility test :** It ensures the sterility status of a product, but instead of on each and every pack, it is performed on sampled packs from the batch. The product is being tested, filtered through membrane filter, which is then transferred to a sterile media and incubated at defined temperature and period of time. The test result, either + ve or – ve, depend on growth of micro-organisms.

  Additives like antimicrobials and certain drugs like antibiotics and sulphonamides may produce false results. The effect of such substances antagonise by doing dilutions and using penicillase, PABA respectively.

  The procedure of test is performed by strictly adopting aseptic techniques under Laminar flow air bench in a sterile area.

- **Pyrogen test :** Pyrogens are metabolic products of living or dead micro-organisms. Chemically pyrogens are lipo-polysaccharides, which cause rise in body temperature after administration.

  The I.P. pyrogen test is done on selected healthy rabbits of either sex. It is performed in two stages :

  (i) Preliminary test : It is known as "sham test" carried out on rabbits, which are being used for pyrogen test for the first time or the animals not used from previous two weeks, is done to condition the rabbits.

  It is performed for 1-3 days by giving a warmed solution of either SWFI or sterile saline at a dose of 10 ml/kg body weight. Recording of body temperature prior to 90 min. for 3 hrs. is done. If any rabbit shows a difference of $0.6^\circ C$ or more then it is not used for the test.

  (ii) Main test : It is performed initially on a group of three rabbits. They are placed into a animal holder box. A thermometer or probe is inserted into the rectum. The product being tested is warmed at $38^\circ C$ then it is injected in the ear's marginal vein of the rabbit. Before the administration of the product the initial temperature, which is the mean temperature recorded at 60 and 90 min is recorded. The recording is continued to further 3 hrs. at an interval of 30 min. The maximum temperature is recorded during the observation. Finally the response is calculated by subtracting the initial temperature from maximum temperature shown by the animal after the injecting the test solution.

(iii) **LAL** : It means "Limulus Amebocyte Lysate", is a another vitro type of test performed to detect pyrogens and bacterial endotoxin of gram negative bacteria.

Principle : Proenzyme $\xrightarrow{\text{Endotoxin}}$ Coagulase

Coagulogen $\xrightarrow{\text{Coagulase}}$ Coagulin (clot)

If pyrogens or bacterial endotoxins, present in the sample to be tested then it is combined with Lysate of horse shoe crab to form coagulase. Coagulase hydrolize, a specific bond of coagulogen protein, present in the blood. Let's produce the gelatinous clot.
(i.e. Coagulin).

Conditions to be fullfilled by Parenteral preparation :

Parenterals are the preparations, those are directly injected into the blood. Hence, they must be harmless i.e. free from physical contaminations, chemical incompatibilities and biological toxins. Therefore, conditions to be fulfilled by parenterals are :

(i)   It should be a clear solution.
(ii) It must be free from solid and liquid particles.
(iii) It shall be free from inert gases.
(iv) It must be isotonic with plasma.
(v)   It must be clinically compatible with other added substances and container.
(vi) The solution must be non-toxic and non-irritant.
(vii) The solution must be enough stable physically and chemically.
(viii) It must be non-pyrogenic.
(ix) It must be a sterile one.

MANUFACTURING OF NON-STERILE PRODUCTS

Definition : Non-sterile manufacturing concern with fibrication of dosage forms except parenterals which is carried out according to standards laid down under schedule M and N of D & C Act 1945.

Non-sterile products include oral liquids, syrups, emulsions, tablets, capsules and suppositories, which are largely consumed. The use products have quite longer shelf life and the manufacturing is less complicated than parenterals. But like parenterals, premises, space machinaries etc. the requirements given under "Schedule M and N" of the Drug and Cosmetic Act 1945, must be complied to manufacture these dosages forms.

Bulk concentrate :

Bulk concentrates are of two types i.e. liquids and semisolids. Liquid concentrates include syrups and elixirs, whereas emulsions, paste, jellys, suppositories and ointments are the semisolid ones.

Solutions of these formulations are prepared in advance by dissolving water soluble ingredients. Sorbitol and parabens may be added. Finally a flavouring agent is added and the solution is filtered after preparing the final volume of bulk. Suitable dilutions are made and dispensed to the In-patients and outpatients.

The entire procedure is carried in a bulk compounding laboratory with adequate facilities like washing, cleaning, processing and storage. Apart from this one should look at supply of fresh air, temperature and humidity control. The chances of contamination could be reduced by keeping the material in an orderly manner with adequate and proper labelling.

Liquid Orals :

Liquid orals are classified as follows :

(i) Simple solutions
(ii) Emulsions
(iii) Suspensions

Advantages :

(i) Quick availability for absorption.
(ii) Irritant substances in dry form to G.I. tract can be given e.g. Bromides and Iodides.
(iii) Easy administration to infants and geriatric patients.
(iv) Assurance of uniform dosage, as it is homogenous, except emulsion and suspension.
(v) The dose can easily vary.
(vi) Hygroscopic drugs can only be given in liquid form.

Disadvantages :

(i) Less stable than solid dosage form.
(ii) Chances of bacterial contamination.
(iii) Rate of degradation is faster than solid dosage form.
(iv) Pleasant odour and taste may result in over dosage with children, which is dangerous.

Manufacturing of Liquid Orals :

Manufacturing of liquid orals must comply the facilities and requirements specified under schedule "M and N" of Drug and Cosmetic Act 1945.

Liquid orals are used for Internal and External purposes.

- **Internal liquids** : Are oral solutions, Elixirs, syrups, drops, draughts, linctuses etc.
- **External liquids** : Liniments, lotions, enemata etc.

Preparations of Internal Liquids :

1. **Vehicles** : Commonly used vehicles are summarised in the following table :

Sr. No.	Nature of Vehicle	Examples
1.	Simple water	Purified water
2.	Aromatic water	Chloroform water Peppermint water Cinnamon water Dill water
3.	Syrups	Simple syrup Orange syrup
4.	Glycerites	Glycerine
5.	For Elixirs	Hydro-alcohols.

2. **Additives** : These are added for flavour and preservation of a solution.

Sr. No.	Nature of Vehicle	Examples
1.	Flavours	Lemon – spirit and compound orange spirit. Compound orange spirit
2.	Preservative	Chloroform, Benzoic Acid, Parabens

Preparation of Linctus :

Linctus is a cough preparation, containing expectorants in a vehicle of simple syrup. These are prepared by steering the medicament in a vehicle, colours, flavours and preservatives are added with agitation in an orderly manner.

Preparation of Elixirs:

Elixirs are clear, flavoured and sweetened hydro-alcoholic liquids. The nature of ingredients is as under :

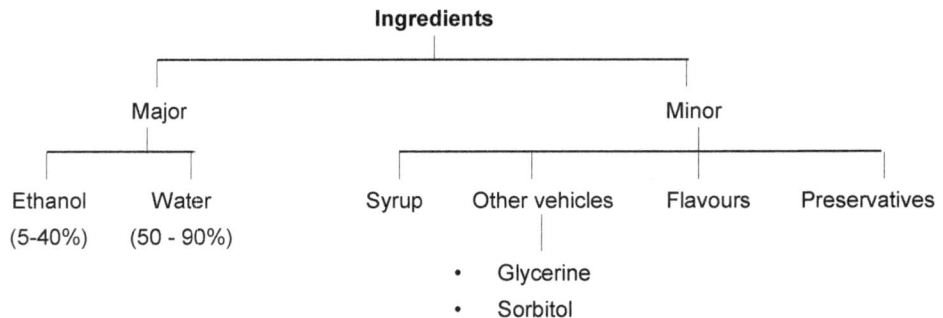

These are prepared by simple way of dissolving two or more ingredients. Aqueous soluble medicament dissolved in water, whereas non-aqueous in alcohol. The aqueous phase is slowly added to alcoholic solution with continuous agitation. Finally, the volume of bulk is adjusted with specified major solvent. If the solution appears turbid allow to stand for few hours and then filter it.

Equipments for liquid orals :
- (i) Storage tank (vehicle)
- (ii) Banded Laboratory's storage tank (for alcohol)
- (iii) Mixing vessels.
- (iv) Portable mixer, small vessels and other utensils.
- (v) Filtration assembly - Filter press, vacuum filters.
- (vi) Bulk storage tank.
- (vii) Filling and packing machineries.

Syrups : Syrups are concentrated aqueous solutions of sucrose or other sugars. They may be viscous in nature and sweet in test. There are mainly of three types :
- (i) Simple.
- (ii) Medicated.
- (iii) Flavoured.

They may be used as :
- (a) Sweetening agents.
- (b) As preservatives.
- (c) As vehicle for :
  * Antitussives
  * Antibiotics
  * Vitamins
  * Analgesics and Antipyretics.

Preparation of Syrups : There are four methods used, which depends on the nature of the syrup being prepared :
1. Solution with heat (General procedure)
2. Agitation without heat : For volatile or thermolabile substances.
3. Addition of medicament to syrup : For extract and tinctures.
4. Percolation : Syrup USP is prepared by this method.

Solution with heat (General Procedure) for production of Syrup

This method is used, when the active ingredients are neither volatile nor thermolabile. A desired quantity of sugar is taken in a petridish and a sufficient amount of purified water is added. Then it is heated on water bath till a solution is obtained. The final volume is made by adding remaining amount of water and heating will continue to obtain a desired viscosity which is tested by "saccharometer". e.g. Syrup I.P.

Preparation of Emulsion

Emulsion is a heterogeneous system in which both the phases - the disperse and continuous phase are liquid. The disperse phase is finely divided in small globules and dispersed in continuous phase with the help of emulgents.

There are three methods used to prepare emulsion :

(i) Dry gum method : Also called 4, 2, 1 method.

(ii) Wet gum method : Also known as English or American method.

(iii) Bottle method.

Dry gum method is commonly used in continent. The ratio of oil, gum and water are taken as 4 : 1 : 2 respectively. Firstly the primary emulsion is produced by stirring gum and oil is adding a small amount of water till a creamy white mass persists. The remaining ingredients are added by dissolving in water slowly in the centre of mortr with continuous agitation.

Manufacture of tablets :

Tablet is a unit solid dosage form containing a medicament with or without pharmaceutical aids, prepared by compressing powdered or granulated form of substances. They are circular disc either with flat or convex surfaces.

Processing of Tablets

Tablet processing comprises mainly with two steps :

(i) Developing the formula.

(ii) Compression of formula.

The methods of compression depends on the nature of ingredients and formula as well. The methods are as follows :

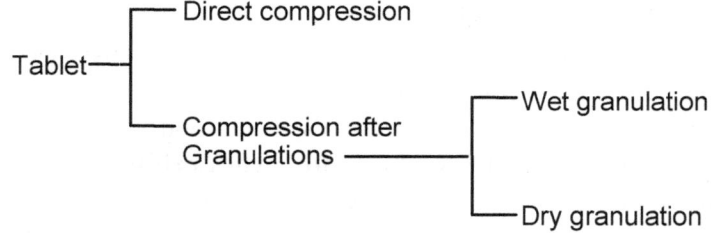

(a) Direct compression : Substances like sodium bromide, sodium chloride, chloral hydrate, Potassium Nitrate and Ferrous glucomate may be compressed either pure or with the addition of disintigrant and lubricant after shifting through a desired sieve directly.

(b) Wet granulation : This process includes weighing of ingredients which are subjected to Grinding and sieving before mixing. Then the bulk is moistened for wet mixing. The entire wet bulk follows for drying to produce the desired size of granules by passing through a sieve. Distintigrants and lubricants are applied to these granules which are then ready for compression.

(c) Dry granulation : Dry granulation is also referred as **"slugging"**. All the ingredients after weighed, grinded and mixed with suitable additives to produce "sluggs" of materials which cannot be granulated by wet drying, having cohesive properties. Then these sluggs are subjected to shifting (sieving) through a desired mesh size. Lubricants are mixed with the particles which are then ready for compression.

Facilities :

Good manufacturing practices, guidelines and FDA Regulations have recommended required section-wise facilities. The different sections of tablet manufacture are as follows :

The temperature and percentage R.H. should be optimum as 25 to 30°C and about 45% RH respectively with exhaust facility.

(i) Weighing Room : It's a small cabinet where weighing of ingredients as per job card is done in pressure of Q.C. chemist.

(ii) Mixing section : The compounding formula is mixed together to reduce the particle size and uniform distribution of all ingredients in the bulk. Then the binding of the bulk is done by adding suitable disintegrator.

(iii) Drying section : The sluggs or moistened bulk is subjected to drying to achieve the hardness and D.T. time under recommended temperature for active medicament.

(iv) Granulating section : Desired mesh is used to obtain particle size for compression and lubricants applied by the stage as well.

(v) Tableting section : It is an air-conditioning rooms for individual machine with storage cabinet for dyes, punches, spanners, brushes, etc.

(vi) Coating section : It is small operational section which needs steam, solution preparation room, pre and post coating storage rooms for tablets.

Equipments :

The equipments required for tablet manufacture recommended under schedule "M" of Drug and Cosmetic Act 1945 are listed in the following table.

Sr. No.	Equipment	Examples
1.	Mixer / Blender	Sigma blade mixer, tumbling mixers, Ribbon blenders.
2.	Grinder / Shifter	Cutter mill, Hammer mill.
3.	Dryers	Tray Dryers, Fluidised bed dryers.
4.	Compression machine	Single punch, Double punch, Rotary etc.
5.	Coating machine	Pan coating, Spray coating pans, Film, Coating machine and Polishing pan etc.
6.	Miscellaneous	S.S. Utensils like scoop, vessels and buckets etc.

Suppositories :

Suppository is a medicated solid dosage form intended for administration in body cavities.

These are used for either local or systemic effects resulting from either melting at body temperature or in mucous secretion.

The methods of preparation are classified as follows :

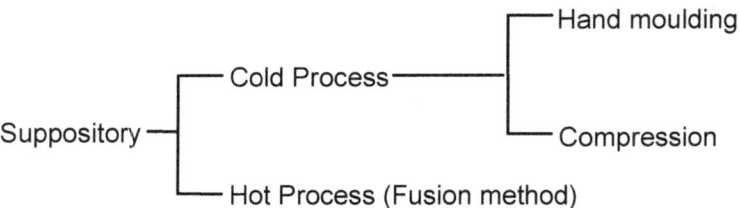

Fusion method : It is the most commonly adopted method which requires muold for any base and lubrication. It involves the following procedure :

(i) Standardisation of mould capacity and amount of base needed as per the displacement value of medicament.

(ii) A base, generally theobroma oil, is taken and melted at 35°C a medicament is added and mixed in porcelain dish on a water bath.

(iii) The above mass is poured in lubricated, cooled moulds and kept in a refrigerator for half and hour to solidification of the suppositories.

(iv) The excess surface is trimmed off, the moulds are opened to eject the suppositories by loosening the screws with gentle pressure from the bottom.

(v) Finally, the individual suppository wrapped with butter paper and placed in carton to dispense.

QUESTIONS

1. What are the factors which determine manufacture of drug within the hospital pharmacy ? **[(S - 03) 4 Marks]**
2. Give methods of estimation of demand. **[(S - 04, 02, 97) 4 Marks]**
3. Name the types of glasses used to prepare containers. Explain the principle involved in hydrolytic resistance test. **[(S - 02, 97) 4 Marks]**
4. Plastic containers used for I.V. Infusion **[(S - 01) 4 Marks]**
5. What is Laminar flow ? **[(S - 02, 02, 97, 96 : W - 02) 4 Marks]**
6. Air Lock. **[(S - 04 : W - 01) 1 Mark]**
7. What do you mean by aerosol disinfection ? Give the names with percentage strength of disinfectant solutions.
8. What is fumigation ? **OR**
   Write a short note on fumigation.
9. Describe layout of sterile products area. **[(S - 01 : W - 98, 96) 4 Marks]**
10. Describe in short the processing involved in sterile/svp manufacturing . **[(S - 01 : W - 99, 00) 4 Marks]**
11. Draw a floor plan of sterile product area. **[(S - 04, 02, 01, : W - 03, 01) Mark - 4]**
12. Name two preservatives used in injections. **[(S - 02, 01, 97 : W - 97) 2 Marks]**
13. What are the various additives used in parenterals. **[(S - 97) 4 Marks]**
14. Give conditions to be fulfilled by all parenterals preparations. **[(S – 01) - 4 Marks]**
    OR
    Explain pyrogen test.
15. What is bulk concentrate ? **[(S - 04, W - 01) 4 Marks]**
16. What are the advantages and disadvantages of liquid orals ? **[(W - 03) 4 Marks]**
17. What is manufacture of liquids orals ? **[(S - 99) 4 Mark]**
    OR
    What are the facilities of equipments required for manufacturing of liquids orals. **[(S - 03) 4 Marks]**
18. What is the general procedure for production of syrup ? **[(W - 00, S - 97) 4 Marks]**
19. What is manufacturing of a drug ? Name equipment for manufacturing tablet. **[(S - 99, 97 : W - 02, 09) 4 Marks]**
20. How suppositories are prepared by fusion process ? **[(S - 98, 00 : W - 96, 99) 4 Marks]**

■■■

6

SURGICAL INSTRUMENTS, MEDICAL EQUIPMENTS AND HEALTH ACCESORIES

(Arms of Surgeon)

INTRODUCTION

Surgical instrument is a term applied collectively to all those instruments used during surgery. Now-a-days the expansion of advanced technology helps the surgeon to fulfill the needs of surgery, implantation or replacement with artificial organs. No surgeon will succeed without taking the aid of surgical instruments.

(A) **Surgical Instruments :** There are numerous instruments available which are used for different activities like incision, cutting, holding, etc. as under :

1. **Scalpels :** The scalpel is a blade with inter-changeable handle system. The blades are of different shapes by which they are named.

Straight   Pointed

Bellied   Bubound

Uses : Scalpels are used to make an incision.

2. **Scissors :** Scissors is a cutting instrument which is generally short and long with different shapes helping in cutting and dissecting.

(a) **Straight Pointed Scissors :**

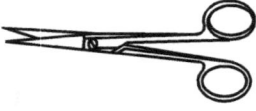

Straight pointed scissors are used freely at places where there is no risk of injury to vital structures.

(b) **Straight Blunt Scissors :**

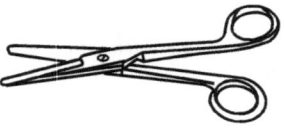

Straight blunt scissors is used where there is a risk of damaging important structure.

(c) Curved on Flat Scissors :

Curved on flat scissors is used in the deep region, where the space is very much confined.

(d) Angle on Edge Scissors :

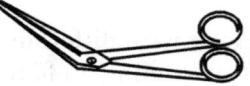

Angle on edge scissors is used to dissect structures which run obliquely.

3. **Tissue forceps :** Tissue forceps are used to hold tissues for traction or opposition, having good grip on the tissues. There are of two types i.e. toothed and un-toothed.

(a) Allis tissue forceps :

It is short and delicate with little gap between the teeth. It is also called as toothed forceps.

Uses : It is used to hold thinner structures like stomach, intestine, rectus sheath and fibrous tissue.

(b) Lanes' tissue forceps :

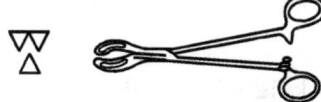

It is long with sharp teeth and stout with a wide gap between the blades.

Uses : It is used to hold tough structures like skin, coarse muscles and tissues.

(c) Rutherford Morison tissue forceps :

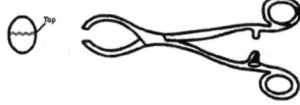

Its teeth are sharp. It was originally used to hold the peritoneum and so called peritoneum forceps.

Uses : It is used to hold fibrous tissue, rectus sheath and stomach.

(d) Babcoks tissue forceps : It is untoothed forcep, the blades are fenestrated.

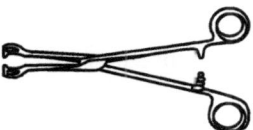

Uses : 1. Used to hold delicate structures and soft tissues.
2. It is used to hold the appendix during appendicestomy.
3. To hold stomach and intestine at the time of gastrojejunostomy.

4. Haemostatic forceps :

Haemostatic forceps are called as artery forceps. These have a special design on the blades like transverse serrations and fenestration, which prevent slipping of the held tissue and crush the blood vessel. The tunica intima curls into lumen and other layer of blood vessel i.e. media and externa blot out the lumen and thus prevents bleeding to achieve haemostatis.

Haemostatic forceps are either short and long with different shapes like straight curved. Ordinary forceps have tooth too. They are mainly of four types.

1. Ordinary forceps
2. Kocher's forceps
3. Lane's forceps
4. Mosquito forceps

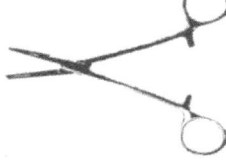

Uses :

1. To achieve haemostatis.
2. To catch bleeding of periosteal vessel.
3. To hold bleeding in fibrous background.
4. In appendectomy to pass ligature around the appendicular artery.

5. Swab holding forceps :

It is long with blades, expanded at the ends where there are transverse serrations and central fenestration which helps to hold swab.

Uses :

(i) To hold fundus of gall bladder during cholecystectomy.
(ii) As a tongue holding forceps.
(iii) For swabbing a cavity.
(iv) To hold ovum.

6. Moynihan's forceps :

It is also known as tetra forceps because of four teeth, two on each side of the blade.

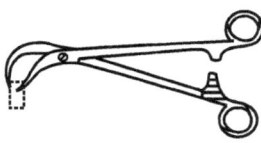

Uses :

(i) Used to fix towel on either side of the incision to the skin to prevent infection.

(ii) Used in abdominal surgery to fix abdominal region.

7. Protoscope :

It is made of stainless steel material comprising the top a hemisphere shaped attached to the rod. The lower part is wider having grooves with smooth rounded end. It facilitates in piercing.

Uses :

- To examines piles.
- To observe fissure and fistula.

Protoscope

8. Blunt currate or Anterior vaginal wall retractor :

It is a gynacological instrument needed to the gynacologist. It is flat, thin slightly wider in the middle region. Both the ends consists of oval shaped rings with hole.

Uses :

- To examine vaginal cavity.
- It can also be used to lift up the vaginal wall.
- It is also used for MTP (Medical termination procedure)

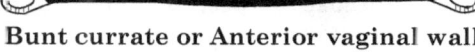

Bunt currate or Anterior vaginal wall rectractor

9. Sharp currate :

It resembles with the blut currate except the size and shape of the rings. These are small and almost elongated oval shaped.

Uses :

- It is used for the dilation of cervix.
- For uterine currate.

Sharp currate

10. Cusco's speculum :

It is a female gonadal instrument, mainly used to retract the vaginal walls for examination of internal structures.

The speculum consists of two blades and a central apperture with screw roller system to widen the blades.

Uses :
- Used to examine vagina.
- To observe the status of cervix and its diseases like cancer or wounds or bacterial infections.
- It is also used to examine copper 'T' (IUCD) position in the vagina.

Screw : To wider the arms by screwing.

Arms : Are the flat, blunt plates.

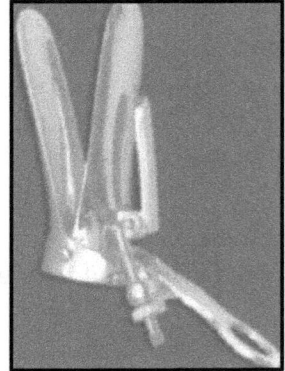

Cusco's speculum

11. Towel Clip :

Uses :

(i) To hold the corners of dressing sheets.

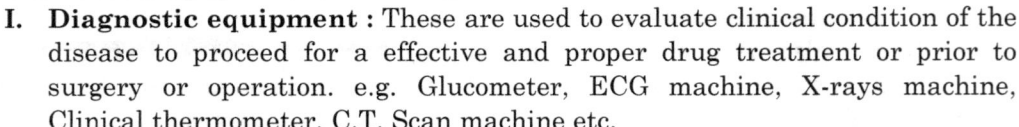

(ii) To fix a sucker tube.

(B) Medical Equipment :

The medical equipment can be categorised as :

I. **Diagnostic equipment :** These are used to evaluate clinical condition of the disease to proceed for a effective and proper drug treatment or prior to surgery or operation. e.g. Glucometer, ECG machine, X-rays machine, Clinical thermometer, C.T. Scan machine etc.

II. **Therapeutic equipment :** These are used to obtain relief from localised or systemic discomfort like pain, swelling or respiratory obstruction. e.g. Nebulizer, Steam vapourizer, Hot water bags etc.

1. Glucometer :

Glucometer is used to check blood sugar level. Blood sugar level has a great significance to maintain the homeostatis of the body. Either increase or decrease in blood sugar (Glucose) level is dangerous for health, it causes disorder known as hyperglycemia i.e. commonly called as Diabetes or hypoglycemia i.e. decrease in blood sugar level.

Now-a-days a variety of compact glucometers are available. So, a diabetic patient need not worry about checking his blood sugar level at outside laboratories. He himself can do it at home and then refer to his physician for further instructions.

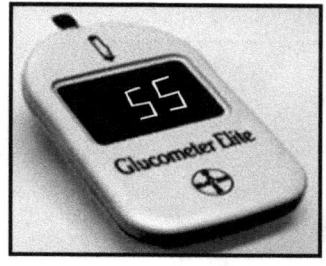

The compact Glucometer can be operated by a single button only by using a strip and the results are obtained within a minute with all details on a display section of Glucometer. Such meters are very easy to handle anywhere by keeping in the pocket.

Glucometer

2. ECG Machine :

A graphical record of electric changes occuring during the cardiac cycle of the heart is known as electrocardiogram (ECG). The instrument used to record ECG is known electrocardiograph.

Principle of ECG : If a U shaped magnet having two pole and a magnetic field is created in that area. In this area a wire is placed which is connected to the battery and the galvanometer. The needle shows deflection which will depend upon the voltage and direction the current. The same phenomenon is applied in the machine.

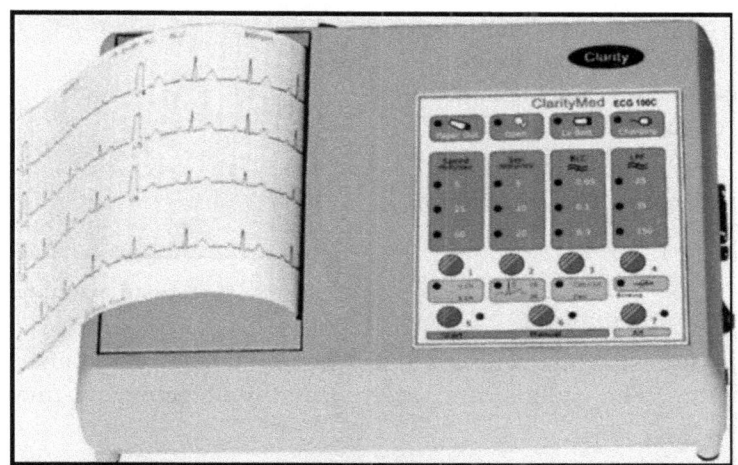

ECG

ECG machine is used to observe the functioning of heart. As the heart problems are increasing day-by-day, ECG machine is a must for all hospitals. Multi-channel ECG analyser machine are available with the hospitals which give complete ECG interpretation and precise recording for accurate and instant diagnosis. Company's like Hinditron and BPL are providing such machine to the hospitals.

3. X-ray machine :

X-ray machine is commonly used as diagnostic tool to observe the condition of the internal structure of the body. For e.g. to check a fracture of bone or condition of lungs to see attack and status of tuberculosis.

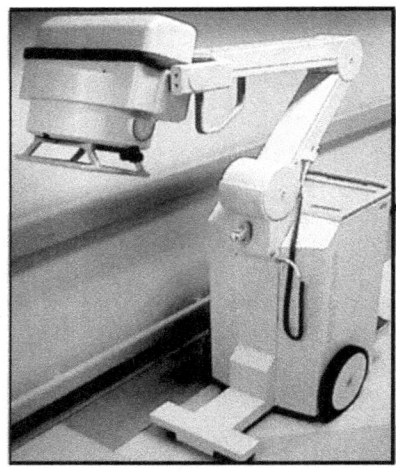

X-rays machine

This machine is operated under radiology section of the hospital. A qualified radiologist and his technicians trained handle it.

4. C.T. Scan machine :

C.T. Scan stands for computed Tomography. It is an advanced technique used for morphological examination of neurological organs, head, eyes, neck, spinal cord etc.

C.T. Scan machine has important components like

(a) Rays generating beam.
(b) Detectors and digitals.

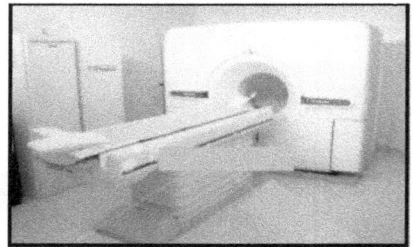

C.T. Scan machine

The x-rays are sharply generated by the electronic beam and focused on a targeted structure. The signals are received by the detector and finally digitalised to store in a memory unit.

5. Clinical Thermometer :

Clinical thermometer is used to measure the body temperature. The temperature inside the body is defined as core temperature. It remains almost constant $\pm 1^{\circ}F$ except when a individual develops a fibril illness.

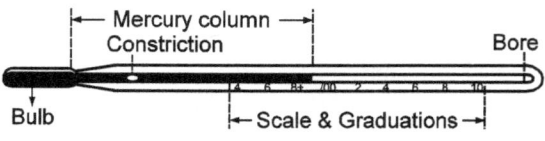

Clinical Thermometer

It is also called fever thermometer and there are three types :

(a) Oral type
(b) Rectal type
(c) Universal type

(a) Oral type : It is characterised by the slender mercury bulb. It is very sensitive for oral use.

(b) Rectal type : It has a strong blunt pear shaped bulb for safety and to retain in the rectum.

(c) Universal type : It can be used for oral as well as rectal use. It is commonly used for children and un-cooperative patients.

All clinical thermometers have a magnifying lens. The back side is opaque. Some have coloured lens which helps in detecting mercury line.

6. Nebulizer :

Nebulizers are used for administration of medicine in disorders of Larynx, trachea and lungs as well as different types of obstructive diseases of the respiratory system.

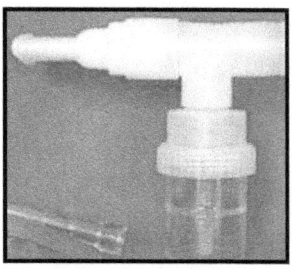

Nebulizer

The nebulizers generate fine particles of liquid in vapours. Within the container of this apparatus a small unit generates automization inside the flask. A flow of air carries mist through the outlet tube of nebulizer.

Ultrasonic nebulizers are also available, which are operated by an electric power. The electric current generates vibrations in the form of waves, that breaks the fluid into the aerosol particles of a range of about 0.5 to 3 μm.

7. Steam vapourizer :

It is an electrically operated device, in which steam is generated with the help of very small heaters. The main advantage of this is that, a constant temperature has been maintained. It is equipped with a regulator, so that when it run dry the heating unit shuts off simultaneously. It is very handy to operate in the home, especially at night.

It is used extensively in the homes, today by the community on the advice of physician to obtained the relief of upper respiratory illnesses, such as colds, sinusitis etc.

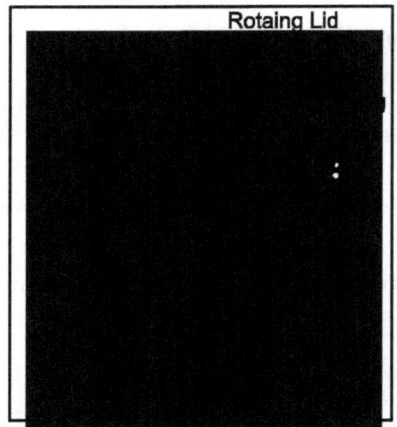

Steam vapourizer

8. Ventilator :

Providing oxygen therapy is a supportive adjunct to the respiratory therapist. Oxygen is the first gas which has therapeutic value, therefore supplemental oxygen is used to treat various clinical disorders, both respiratory and non-respiratory in nature. Generally, 2L/min O_2 is needed to get relief of arterial hypoxemia, and therapeutically, it is provided to treat pulmonary hypertension and polycythemia, by keeping a patient on ventilator.

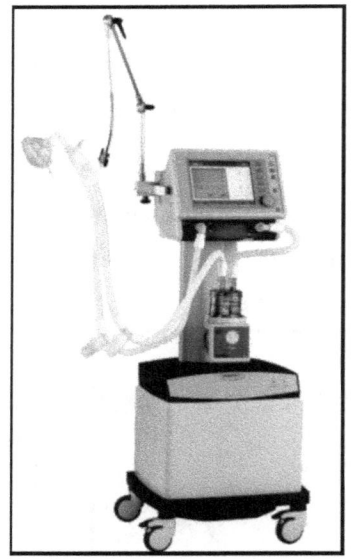

Ventilator

9. Oxygen Concentrator or Enricher :

It is an electrically operated device consisting pump, which forces the ambient room air through a semipermeable membrane, that separates the nitrogen and delivers about 95% of oxygen at a rate of 3 to 5 L/min. This system never needs re-filling and most convenient to those patients, who are homebound. The only drawback of the equipment is that, it produces certain amount of noise.

Oxygen Concentrator or Enricher

10. Apnea monitor :

The great threat to the lifehood of infants is due to sudden infant death syndrome, which is characterised by pause in respiration of 15-20 seconds or longer. This is some what similar to the symptoms of apnea. This is the greatest challenge to medical community, and hence the hospital authorities started apnea monitoring program by framing a committee of respiratory therapists, under the guidance of a Neonatologist.

Apnea monitor

Apnea monitoring is done by pneugrams (pneumocardiogram) by using a device, so called Apnea monitor, which provides two channel recordings of respiration and heart rate. These typically can be done at home for 12 hours period. Then these recordings are printed out and analysed by the physician or respiratory therapist, for further care.

11. Hot water bottles :

Hot water bottles are used to get relief from the localised muscular pain. The bottles are made up of rubber with a capacity of about 500 ml. A cloth is wrapped around the bottle to get comfort from hot water.

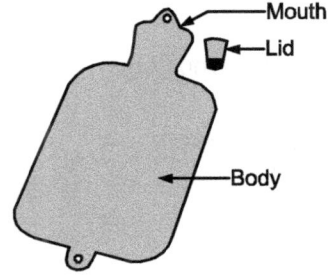

Hot water bottle

(C) Health Accessories :

Numerous health accessories are used in the hospital for rehabilitation, restoration and maintenance of life style. These are two types :

I. Ambulatory aids :

    e.g.   Wheel chair

              Walkers

              Canes and crutches etc.

II. Bed-side aids :

    e.g.   Cot with bed and swing

              Infusion bottle stand

              Bed-side cabinet etc.

Wheel-chairs :

A chair with wheels used for patients unable to walk. Different types of wheel chairs are available.

Walkers :

A framework used as a support by patients who cannot walk without one.

Canes and Crutches :

Canes help to transfer the weight of the weak limb and maintain the balance of the body.

List of Surgery

Sr. No.	Surgery	Meaning
A.	**G.I. Tract related :**	
	Gastgroenterotomy	A surgical incision into the stomach and intestine.
	Gastrectomy	A removal of portion or the entire stomach.
	Ostomy	A surgical procedure, in which a portion of intestine or urinary tract is removed, to allow the passage faeces or urine.
	Gastrojejunostomy	A surgical creation of an anastomosis between the stomach and jejunum.
	Appendictomy	A surgical procedure is adopted to remove the vermiform appendix.
	Colostomy	In this, the diversion of faecal matter stream is obtained through opening in the colon.
	Cholecystectomy	A surgical procedure applied with gall bladder.

Contd....

B.	**Related to Genitourinary :**	
	Lithotripsy	A procedure in which renal stone is dissolved by lesser beam.
	Calpotomy	An incision is applied to the vagina.
	Ophorectomy	A procedure of removal of ovaries.
	Salpingectomy	An excision of uterine tubes.
	Vasoctomy	A procedure of removal of vas-deference.
	Lithotomy	It is a procedure applied for viginal examination in case of kidnapping.
	Oncotomy	It is a procedure applied to surgery of the tumor.
	Lasix	Laser in situ keratomalacia
	PRK	Photorefractive keratotomy (Procedure applied to correct refractor disorder of eyes)
C.	**Related to haemophoietic :**	
	Carotid enderterectomy	A procedure that includes removal of atheriosclerotic plague from the carotid artery to restore the blood flow of brain.
	Phelebotomy	A procedure of removal of blood to lower the viscosity of blood of a patient with polycythemia.
	Thrombectomy	An operation, to remove blood clot from blood vessels.
D.	**Related to other systems :**	
	Lymphadenectomy	A procedure is adopted to remove the lymph node.
	Pneumonectomy	A procedure of surgical removal of lungs is called as pneumonectomy.

QUESTIONS

1. What is the use of Haemostatic forceps ? [W : 03]
2. What are surgical instruments ? Name any three instruments with uses ?
   [S - 04, 02 : W - 00]
3. Write a note on Glucometer ? [(S - 01, 96) 4 marks]
4. Write a note on ECG machine ? [(S - 01, 96) 4 marks]
5. Write a note on clinical thermometer ?
6. Name two accessories and their uses. [(S - 03) 2 marks]

■■■

7

PHARMACY AND THERAPEUTIC COMMITTEE AND HOSPITAL FORMULARY SYSTEM

(Surveillance of Hospital Activities)

INTRODUCTION

Now-a-days in the era of advanced medicine, when numerous drugs are available for the treatment of different diseases, the rational selection of drugs for use has become very important administratively and therapeutically. For this hospitals make a sound policy for effectiveness and safety. This could be achieved by the constituting pharmacy and therapeutic committee (PTC).

Composition of PTC : The Pharmacy and Therapeutic committee is composed of Representatives from all walks of health care system. It can be elaborated schematically as below :

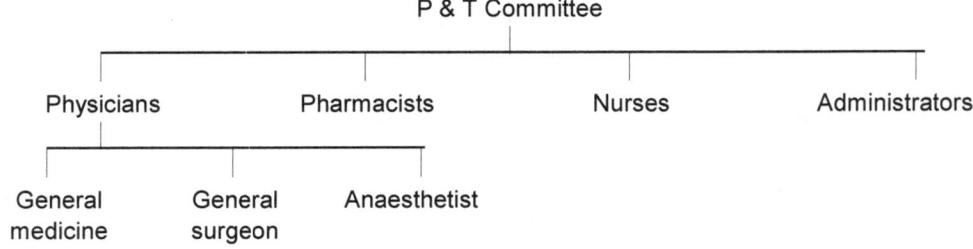

A "chair person" is appointed from physician representative and a pharmacist works as "secretary".

Purpose of PTC : The Pharmacy and Therapeutic Committee works with two main objectives or purposes as below :

1. **Educational :** PTC recommends to organize programmes, seminars or workshops to furnish the current development on matters regarding drugs and safe use.

2. **Advisory :** PTC emphasises on implementation of policies laid down for selection, evaluation and rational use of drug in a hospital.

Agenda of the committee : The success of meeting depends upon the nature of the agenda, which is made available to the members of the committee before scheduling the meeting by the secretary.

A typical agenda may consists of the following points :
- Minutes of previous meeting.
- Review of :
    - Hospital formulary sections either addition or deletion of product.
    - Adverse drug reaction reported in a hospital since the previous meeting.
- Drug safety in a hospital.

The meeting of the committee should be atleast 6 times in a year and whenever necessary. The minutes of the meeting are prepared by the secretary and he is supposed to maintain the records permanently. The recommendations will be presented to the medical staff for their implementation.

Functions and Objectives of P&T Committee :
1. To guide the medical staff and the hospital administration in all matters related to the use of drug.
2. Lay down written policies and procedures for the appraisal, selection, procurement, storage and distribution of drugs.
3. To form the hospitals own formulary and periodically up-date it.
4. Prepare a list of drugs for emergency kit and first aid kit.
5. Prepare a list of drugs to be kept in ward pharmacy, floor stock drug system.
6. Conduct quality audit and check GMP practised at own and other manufacturing units.
7. To review adverse drug reactions to the drug.
8. To establish and promote suitable educational programmes on safe use of drugs in a hospital for all professional staff members.
9. To advise the pharmacy staff to render better services to the out-patients and the in-patients.
10. Arrange periodical workshops, seminars and training programmes for medical staff, pharmacist and nursing including other health care personnels.
11. Form sub-committees if needed to design policies regarding rational therapy for special groups based on pharmacological actions e.g.

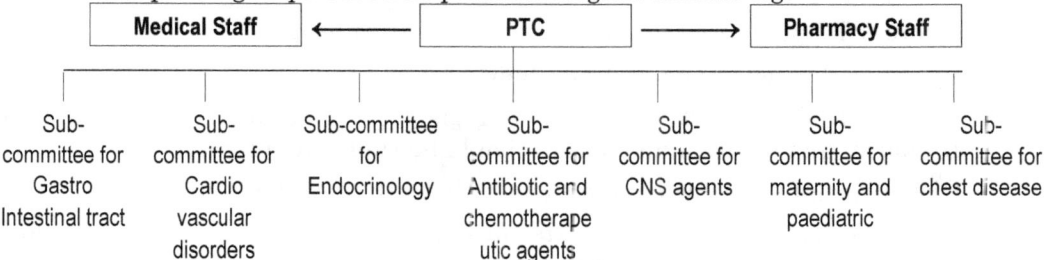

PTC and Adverse Drug Reactions

Sometimes the drug may produce unwanted or unexpected effects. This is called adverse drug reaction. It is a result of overdosage, hypersensitivity or allergic condition.

The committee acts in two ways i.e. to treat such patients and to prevent such happenings in the future. A physician concerned will submit a report for this. A typical format of ADR is as follows :

ADVERSE DRUG REACTION REPORT

Report No. : ....   Date : ....

Name of the Patient : ....

Age : .... Year   Gender : ....   Body weight : .... kg

Therapy followed :

(a) Reported disease / Indication : ....

(b) Drug that produced ADR : ....

(c) Reaction details : .   ...

(d) Sources of drugs :

    (i) Batch No. :   ....

    (ii) Mfg. and Exp. date :   ....

    (iii) Manufacturer :   ....

Steps taken to treat ADR :   ....

Name of attending physician :   ....

Signature of the physician :   ....

Drug Safety and Role of the Committee :

Drug safety is one of the prime responsibilities of the hospital pharmacist. There is a vast advancement of new categories of therapeutic drugs. So, the drug safety aspect being taken for granted by the hospitals professionals in our nation. Pharmacy medication errors or accidents result in serious conditions or lead to the death of the patient.

Therefore, PTC plays a vital role for drug safety in a hospital.

Following guidelines are helpful to achieve it.

1. The chief pharmacist should be a registered pharmacist with minimum B.Pharm. qualification and others should be Diploma holders.

2. Dispensing of medicine shall be done only by the registered pharmacist.

3. Adequate number of pharmacists must be appointed to fulfill the 24 hour working requirements, in different shifts.

4. Adequate, facilities shall be provided for the storage and handling of medicine in the pharmacy.

5. Glass infusion bottles, containers shall not be permitted for other uses like to store antiseptic solution or collect urine etc.

6. Narcotics, psychiatric or poisonous substances should be stored in separate cupboard under lock and key and shall confirm the legal requirements.

7. Quality audit should be carried out at regular frequencies, to check whether the guidelines of GMP are followed.

8. Library and documentation facility shall be provided.

9. No one shall be allowed to enter the pharmacy after closing the house of the pharmacy, except the pharmacist.

HOSPITAL FORMULARY SYSTEM

Hospital formulary can be defined as an important document of the hospital containing a collective list of drugs. This book is used extensively by the interne and fellow doctors. The hospital formulary is to be revised periodically and should reflect the current aspects of the clinical judgements of the medical staff.

The hospital formulary system is a powerful tool for improving the quality and controlling the cost of the drug therapy. The pharmacy therapeutic committee of the hospital is incharge of the preparation and its revision. Physicians own formula, found to be useful, is incorporated into the hospital formulary.

Objectives / Significances of Hospital formulary system :

1. To provide information on which drug products have been approved for the use by PTC.
2. To furnish the staff the basic therapeutic information about each approved drug product.
3. To deliver information on hospital policies and procedures pertaining to the use of drug.
4. To elicit special information of drug about drug dosing, rules and abbreviations used in a hospital.

Limitations of Hospital Formulary System :

1. The system may prevent the physician's right to prescribe and obtain the brand of his choice.
2. The system in many instances permits the pharmacist to act as the sole judge of which brand of medicine is to be purchased and dispensed.
3. The system do not minimise the cost of medicine to the patient by passing discount or any scheme received at the time of purchase in bulk quantity by the hospital.
4. The system may allow purchase of inferior quality medicine, where there is no staff pharmacist.

Nature and appearance of formulary :

The nature and physical appearance of the formulary may influence its use. The formulary should process the following qualities :
- It should be visually pleasant.
- The language should be easily understood.
- Neatness is a must.

There is no unique format which will formularies must follow. A typical formulary may have the following sections.

(i) Title page.

(ii) Name and titles of members of the pharmacy and therapeutic committee.

(iii) Table of contents.

(iv) Details of hospital policies and procedures concerning drugs.

(v) List of approved products that can be used in a hospital.

(vi) A complete list of branded and generic drugs available in the market.

(vii) Prescription writing is an important section for fellow physicians.

(viii) Appendix : It consists of

    (a) Normogram for estimating
- Body weight with relation to height.
- Body surface area.

    (b) Normogram of Blood pressure for various age groups.

    (c) Posological table.

    (d) List of central services and supply.

    (e) Poisons and their antidotes.

Guiding principles of hospital formulary :

The formulary is framed by the medical staff upon the recommendations of PTC. The medical staff should follow the policies and adopt the procedures developed by the PTC, and serve as the guiding principles are summarised below :

(i) It guides on appraisal, selection, procurement and storage of drugs.

(ii) The policies and procedures guide on distribution, safe and rational use of drugs.

(iii) It is a ready reference having information on various aspects like antidote, category-wise list of drugs etc. to retrieve the information in emergency situation.

(iv) It act as a specialised guide to pharmacist, nursing staff and doctors too.

Factors / Criteria's for addition or deletion of new drugs in the formulary :

It is the greatest challenge to the PTC, to frame the gauzes of selecting criteria's for the addition or deletion of drugs or formulations. This is because of the fact that the majority of the members of committee is not so highly qualified to evaluate the clinical or therapeutic efficacy of the drugs; but following factors are being considered, while doing the activity.

- The addition of new drugs in the formulary is purely depends on, whether the drug is found, clinically authentic by either local general practitioner or a speciality staff member. The approval of drug by speciality staff is valuable to incorporate the drug in it.
- The drugs must be recognised by the official books or their supplements.
- The secret formulations may not be added in the formulary.
- The drugs produced by the manufacturer must comply with the recommended standards; if found inferior, such drugs may be deleted.
- A general policy regarding multiple composition of drugs, not to incorporated in the formulary is adopted by majority of hospital.

QUESTIONS

1. Give the composition of PTC. [W - 03 : S - 02]
2. What is PTC ? Give its composition. [(S - 04, 01, 99, 97, 96 : W - 00) 4 marks]
3. Write short note on PTC. [(W - 01) 4 marks]
4. Explain the need and functions of PTC. [(S - 03) 4 marks]
5. How PTC ensures drug safety in a hospital ? [(W - 97) 4 marks]
6. Define hospital formulary. Give its significances. [S - 03, 01, 97 : W - 97]
7. What is hospital formulary ? Give its importance. [W - 03]
8. Write a short note on hospital formulary. [S - 03]

■■■

8

DRUG INFORMATION SERVICES AND DRUG INFORMATION BULLETIN

(The Data Bank)

INTRODUCTION

Drug information is the facility of oral or written information or advice about drug and therapy in response to a demand from other healthcare professionals, organisations, committees, patients or an individual of the public.

Drug Information Services (DIS) explains activities undertaken by the pharmacist in providing information to optimise rational use of drugs.

Now-a-days advanced technology is being used for diagnosis, surgery, therapy and a modern trend in therapeutic management. All these services provided to the health community needs a specific, latest information. Hence a well-organised pharmacy library plays an important role to provide such information.

The pharmacist answers the query through the Drug Information Centre (DIC) or services. He is the right person to head the Drug Information Centre because :

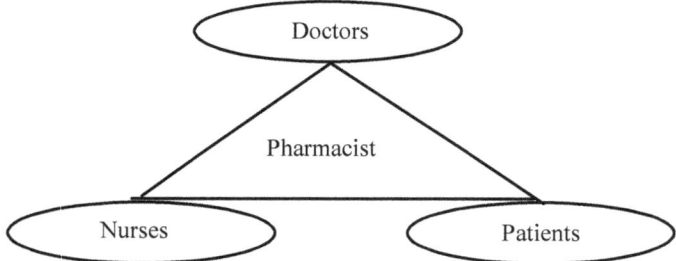

(i) He is the member of the pharmacy Therapeutic committee.

(ii) He knows the sources of information.

(iii) He has the ability to evaluate the literature critically.

(iv) He has the knowledge how to handle computer.

(v) He knows the role of other hospital staff members.

India is a country with significant drug use problems. Irrational and over prescribing is common and antibiotic resistance is widespread. Such problems are as a result of variety of economic, social, medical and regulatory factors. The most important of these include :

1. Lack of awareness about the drug information centre.
2. Availability of tremendous formulations.
3. The national drug policy is industry oriented rather than health oriented.
4. Lack of awareness about the drug's rational use practices among doctors and pharmacists.
5. Increasing sale of prescription drugs over the counter (OTC), despite this being illegal and where there is high level of illiteracy, poverty among patients.

Utility of Drug Information Services (DIS)

1. To present a specific and vital information to the doctors for drug therapy.
2. To guide on :
   (a) Pharmacy research project.
   (b) Education programmes.
   (c) Other pharmacy services such as drug distribution, storage and handling of medicine and advices to the patient etc.
3. To provide regular, periodic amendments on drugs to the medical practitioners.
4. To provide research findings to the physician.
5. To produce comparative information to the doctor that helps him to evaluate potential of new drug for the same treatment.

Sources of Drug Information and Staff

One of the functions of the Pharmacy Therapeutic Committee is to maintain a library and documentation services. The librarian has to collect and sort out all the vital information available with different sources to furnish it, to the hospital staff. The sources are categorised as under :

1. Primary sources :

1. The information obtained from basic researches and developments, which is publicised in brief for the first time.
2. The information available on internet, web sites, C.D. ROM etc.

2. Secondary sources :

Primary information, available in the form of abstracts, journals, periodicals, text books, References and official books is called secondary sources which is given below :

(a) Journals and Periodicals :
- American Journal of Hospital pharmacy.
- The Indian Journal of Hospital pharmacy.
- Journal of American Medical Association.
- Journal of Indian Medical Association.
- Journal of Clinical and Hospital Pharmacy.
- Journal of Clinical Pharmacology.

(b) Text books :
- Textbook of Hospital Pharmacy - Hassan.
- Clinical Toxicology – Lee.
- Pharmacological basis of Therapeutics – Goodman and Gilman.

(c) Reference books :
- Remington's Pharmaceutical Sciences.
- Merk Index.
- Wintrobe's Haematology.

(d) Pharmacopoeias :
- The Indian Pharmacopoeia (I.P.).
- United States Pharmacopoeia (U.S.P.)
- British Pharmacopoeia (B.P.)
- British Pharmaceutical Codex (B.P.C.)

(e) Formularies :
- National Formulary of India (NFI)
- National Formulary of America (NFA)
- British National Formulary (BNF)

Drug Information Bulletin (DIB) :

The drug information centre may publish a journal or periodical or any booklet about current or amended information on drugs, various technical aspects and modernization of hospital practices for all the health professionals, which is referred as "Drug information bulletin".

Advantages of DIB :

- To furnish current information to physicians, pharmacist, nursing staff and fellow candidates of all disciplines.
- It is a link between the Drug information centre and health professionals.
- It helps the hospital staff regarding recent researches and clinical practices.

QUESTIONS

1. What is the utility of DIS ? [S - 03, 02]
2. What are the sources of information for Drug Information Services ?
   [(W - 01, 00 : S - 96) 4 marks]
3. Write a note on DIS or Centre. [(S - 03, 02) 4 marks]
4. What is Drug information bulletin ? [S - 01 : W - 99]

■■■

9

SURGICAL DRESSINGS AND SUPPLIES

(The Medical Devices)

INTRODUCTION

Surgical dressings or curatio is a term applied to materials used for dressings of wounds. These materials are basically employed as protectives, absorbents, protectives or support for the disease for injured tissue.

Properties of Surgical dressings :

(i) It must be porous to water vapours.

(ii) It must be capable of absorbing excess secretion.

(iii) It should not adhere to the wound surface.

(iv) Do not interfere with wound healing.

(v) Do not produce tissue reaction.

(vi) It must be impervious to micro-organisms.

(vii) It must have smooth surface, good tensile strength.

(viii) It must be capable of preventing excessive movement of wounds.

The surgical dressings include :

1. Primary wound dressings.
2. Absorbents.
3. Bandages.
4. Adhesive tapes.
5. Protectives.

1. Primary wound dressings :

These dressings are placed in contact with the wound surface and are usually reinforced by other suitable material. The purpose is to absorb the wound secretion and minimise maceration. e.g. Absorbent gauze or surgical guaze, plain guaze.

Surgical gauze : Also called an absorbent guaze, it is an absorbent material, having sufficient tensile strength for surgical dressing.

It prepared from raw cotton. After cleaning it is spun into a thread. The thread is woven into an open meshed cloth. The cloth is bleached and made absorbent. The mesh size of guaze differs according to the gauze. The absorbent gauze's have a lower mesh size. Some dressing needs a close meshed guaze for greater strength and protection.

Uses :

1. It is used after surgery to drain exudate from major wounds.
2. It is used to pack dental sockets, sinuses etc.
3. To remove debris, pus without damaging tissue.

2. Absorbents :

Absorbents are mainly employed for absorbing blood and fluids of injured tissues and other discharges.

e.g. Surgical cotton,

Eye pads,

Sanitary napkins.

Eye pads : Eye pads are designed in a manner to comfortably cover the eye. The pads are made up of non-woven fabric material. They are provided in a sterile pack.

Sanitary napkins : These are also called V pads, maternity pads and obstetrical pads. These pads have the ability to hold high fluid. The napkin is made of non-woven fabric usually covered by an open mesh scrim. The side and the outer surfaces of the napkin consist of water-repellent material.

3. Bandages :

Bandages are used to hold dressings in place and to provide support or pressure.

e.g. Common guaze roller bandage

Muslin bandage

Elastic bandage

Common gauze bandages :

These are made up of surgical / absorbent type gauze and available in various sizes. They are reasonably free from loose thread.

Muslin bandage :

These are reasonably strong and used where the common guaze bandage does not provide adequate strength or support.

Elastic bandages :

These are of different types and are employed for a specific use.

(a) Woven elastic bandage : These are made of webbing and contain rubber threads. They provide support or strength.

(b) Crape bandage : It does not contain rubber and elastic but can extend to roughly twice its length. The elasticity is due to its special weaving. It is used for bandaging varicose vein.

4. **Adhesive Tapes :**

Adhesive tapes are made of different types varying in both in type and formulation of the adhesive mass depending on the use and requirements. Adhesive tapes are of two types, namely :

(a) Rubber-based adhesive tapes.

(b) Acrylated adhesive tapes.

These two types are employed in different conditions. Rubber based adhesive tapes are cheaper and used when maximum adhesiveness and backing strength is required. Acrylated adhesive tapes are mainly used in operative and post-operative surgical, dressings, where minimum skin Trauma is required.

e.g. Zinc oxide adhesive plaster

Capsicum plaster

Belladona plaster

Belladona and capsicum plaster.

5. **Protectives :**

Protectives are employed with different purposes like to cover wet dressings and poultices. It is also used to retain heat, in hot or cold compress. They also prevent escape of moisture from the wet dressings and compress. Protectives commonly are of plastic sheeting, rubber sheeting or coated papers with wax or plastic.

Absorbent Cotton

Absorbent cotton consists of the epidermal trichomes of the seeds of the cultivated species of *Gossypium herbeceum, Gossypium barbadence* and other species.

Preparation of Cotton :

Raw cotton is obtained by collection from 3 to 5 celled capsule (bolls) containing numerous seeds, is subjected to the process of combing whereby short fibres are separated and used for preparation of absorbent cotton. This process is called "gining".

The short fibres, known as "comber" waste, are boiled for 10 to 15 hours with dilute caustic soda solution, under 1 to 3 atmospheric pressure to remove the natural waxes and colouring matters this is called saponification.

Bleaching is done with chlorinated soda and then treated with dilute hydrochloric acid. Finally it is washed with water to remove excess of alkali. Finally drying is done to recard into flat sheets. It is packed into packages and usually sterilised with eto.

Packing : Packaging is done by rolling the packages of not more than 0.5 kg of a continuous lap with thin paper running with the entire lap and sealed in well closed container.

Description : Absorbent cotton occurs as a white soft, fine filament like hairs. The hairs are unicellular, 2.5 to 4.5 cm in length and 40 µm wide. It is colourless and odourless. It offers appreciable resistance when pulled and does not shed a significant quantity of dust.

It is used for surgical dressing purpose, hence should qualify the standard of evaluation as per Indian Pharmacopoeia.

I. **Identification test :** A single fibre of absorbent cotton is examined under linear microscope to measure the length and the diameter along with the shape.

II. **Chemical test :**

   (a) Treatment with iodinated zinc chloride solution fibre becomes violet and is observed under the microscope.

   (b) Treatment with zinc chloride solution : Fibres are boiled with solution at 40°C for $2\frac{1}{2}$ hrs. They do not dissolve.

III. **Acidity or Alkalinity :** Macerate is used to check the pH by using methyl red or phenolphthalein solution as an indicator. Neither solution shows a pink colour.

IV. **Absorbency test :** This test is evaluated by performing sinking time test and water holding capacity. The I.P. limits for sinking time, not more than 10 sec. and for water holding capacity, not less than 23 gm of water per gm of sample.

V. **Fluorescence :** A 5 mm thickness layer is observed under 365 nm u.v. lamp. It shows only a slight brownish violet fluorescence and few yellow particles. Not more than few fibres show an intense blue fluorescence.

VI. **Neps :** A sample is spread on 450 sq. cm. area glass plate and covered with another plate. The Neps are observed by the naked eye and marked with glass pencil. The limit is not more than 250 neps.

VII. **LOD :** Means 'loss on drying' and is performed to check the % w/w volatile and moisture substances. IP limit is not more than 8% w/c at 105°C in oven.

VIII. Sulphated Ash : Not more than 0.5% w/w. It is performed to determine the substances on ignition.

Apart from these other tests are also given in the monograph of the Indian pharmacopoeia.

Surgical Supplies : Generally the services given by many pharmacies, consisting of supply of catheters, B.D. sets Ryel's tube, I.V. and B.T. set and other equipment needed by the surgeon are as under :

1. Catheters :

Catheters are used to collect urine from the patients unable to void naturally or have trouble of incontinence pants or external catheters are not adequate.

Catheters are of two types :

(a) Rubber catheters : There are different types and sizes of catheters made up of rubber tubes with a closed tip and are flexible in nature. The other end is open, having a funnel shape, which is attached to another tube of the collection unit. At the inserted end there is a wide hole which acts as a channel to flow the urine.

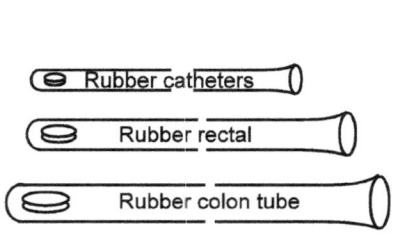 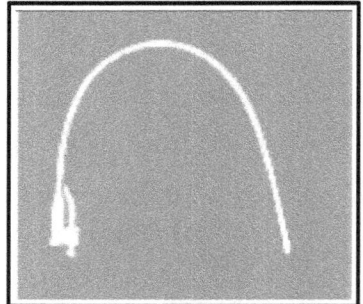

Fig. 9.1

(b) Foley catheters : It is commonly known as **"balloon catheters"**, because at its inserting end it has a balloon.

Fig. 9.2

The balloon provides safety to the tip of the catherter in patients bladder. The balloon has the capacity from 5 or 30 ml. The 30 ml catheter, also called as **Hemostatis catheter**, is used for dialysis purposes in clinics.

2. B.D. Set :

B.D. set stands for "Beckton and Dickinson" who manufactured it. It consists of a syringe and a needle.

It is a glass syringe which could be sterilised by autoclaving. The B.D. needle has bevel, body and shoulder it can be locked in a syringe by applying metallic lever lock to the nozzle.

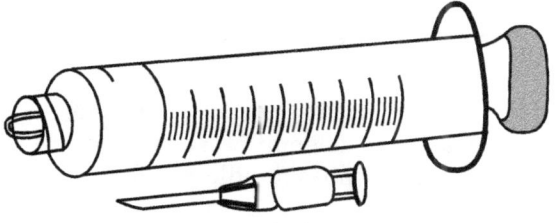

Fig. 9.3 : B.D. Set

Uses :

1. It is used to collect fluids from the body cavity.
2. It could be used to collect blood from the doner.
3. It is used to administer the drug by I.M. route.

3. Ryle's tube :

It is a thin tube having the length of about 30 inches. Distally there is an oral bulb, which provides the swallowing of the tube. Above the bulb there are "4" small holes through which liquid can be poured into the stomach or aspirated from it. The tube has siliconised and smooth outer surface to reduce chances of tissue irritation.

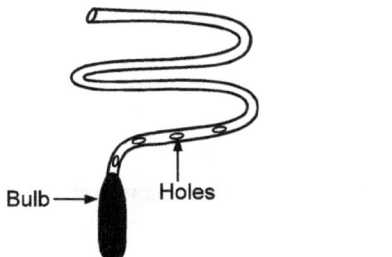 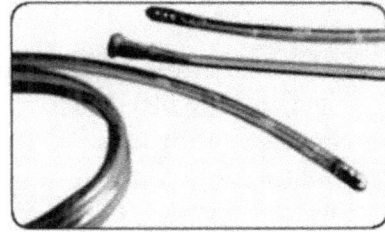

Fig. 9.4 : Ryle's tube

Uses :

1. To give fluid or drugs to those patients who can't imbibe enough quantity.
2. To give stomach wash in case of poisoning.
3. For gastric juice analysis.
4. To deflate the stomach in case of GIT obstruction.

4. B.T. Set :

Means blood transfusion set. It is made up of plastic, sterile and its pathway is non-pyrogenic. It is non-toxic and for single use only.

The B.G. (B.T.) set consists of various parts as under :

1. **Spike with cover :** The tip of the spike is sharp and tapering which helps in piercing into the mouth of the blood bag. It is protected with a cover, which is made of LDPE material to prevent the contact with environment.

2. **Drip chamber :** It is made of polypropylene or polyethylene and acts as a small reservoir for the blood. It consists of a filter in its middle portion.

3. **Filter :** A nylon made basket like hollow bag is fixed into a drip chamber. All blood components are leucocyte - depleted within 48 hours of the collection of blood. This helps to minimise the theoretical risk of transmission of VCJD.

4. **Roller clamp :** It is made of HDPS or ABS plastic material. The wheel of the clamp regulates the flow rate, which is generally kept 20 drops per min ± 0.1 ml.

5. **Tubing :** It is transparent and soft one with a length of about 6.0 feet. It serves as a pathway polyethylene or poly-vinyl chloride is used to prepare it.

6. **Cannula :** It is a blind opening provided for the administration of a specific blood component at the time of transfusion.

7. **Injection site :** A latex tube portion is provided with the tubing to inject the drug with blood.

8. **Needle holder :** It provides the site to fix the needle.

9. **Needle :** A hypodermic needle is supplied with the set which is prefixed and inserted into the vein.

10. **Needle protector :** Plastic cap covers the needle to prevent the contact of atmosphere with it.

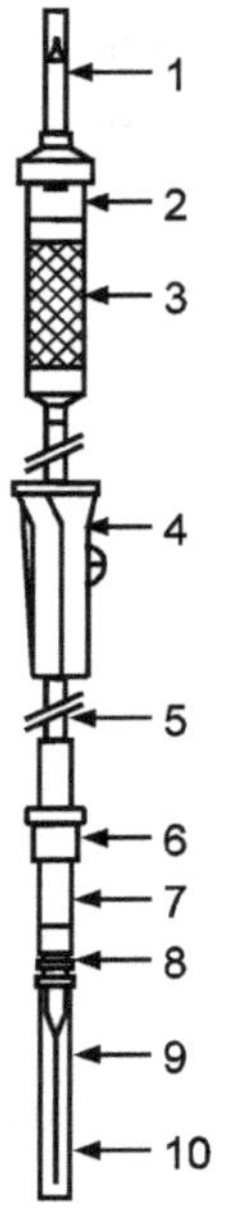

Fig. 9.5 : Blood transfusion set

5. I.V. set :

It stands for intravenous solution administration set. Since **I.V. set** is a life-saving devicely. It is declared "Drug" in the special notification by the Govt. of India.

Requirements of an Ideal I.V. set :

1. It should be sterile and non-pyrogenic.
2. It should be free from particulate matter.
3. It should be easy in handling.

I.V. set is used to administered large volume of parenterals. It consists of various components which are made up of different types of materials as mentioned below :

1. **Spike cover :** It protects the spike and maintains its sterility from external environment. It is made up of LDPE plastic.
2. **Spike :** It helps in piercing the closure or cap of the bottle. The spike is made up of ABS, its tip is tapering and sharp.

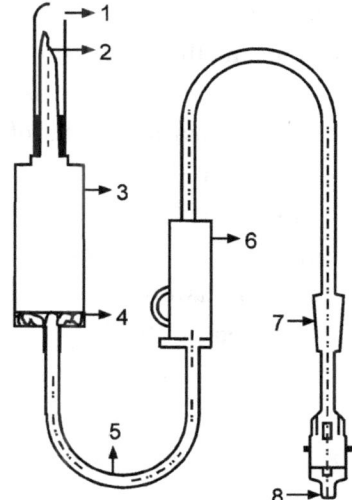

Fig. 9.6 : Intra-venous set

3. **Drip chamber :** It acts as a small reservoir for solution. It is transparent and squeezable. This property helps in preventing air bubbles from entering the fluid path. The chamber is made up of polypropylene.
4. **Filter :** It is placed at the bottom of drip chamber. It is made up of nylon having pore size of 15 μ.
5. **PVC Tubing :** The tube is colourless, soft and transparent, having a length of 150 cm. with an internal diameter of 2.7 min. It acts as a pathway.
6. **Flow Regulator :** It has two parts namely : (a) Body, (b) Wheel. Body supports the movement of the wheel. This controls the flow rate. Body and wheel is made up of HDPS and ABS plastic respectively.
7. **Injection site :** It is made up latex. SVP can be given to the patient via this site when he is on I.V. fluid therapy.
8. **Adapter :** It is the distal end connection site for needle. It is made of PP plastic.
9. **Needle :** It is provided with each pack of I.V. set. It is covered with cup, which is made up of polypropylene.

Safety test : I.V. set is a polymeric product, essentially have to qualify the biological test to ensure its safety for using as an auxillary for intravenous administration. The test is performed as follows :

Procedure : A single I.V. set selected from an entire produced batch. The set is then filled completely with 0.9% w/v sodium chloride injection, both the ends of the set are clamped to prevent drainage of filled solution. The filled set is then emmersed in autoclave containing water and heated at 80°C for an hour. After this the filled solution collected and finally injected by I.V. route to five healthy mice at a dose of 0.5 ml. Then these animals are observed for next 4, 24 and 48 hours. The animal does not show any descernible signs of toxicity, if so, then the I.V. set is said to be safe for using as an auxillary for I.V. administration.

Safety tests for infusion assemblies :

The infusion fluid travels through the infusion set (assembly) during its transfusion, must be as pure as the infusion is, to prevent the possibility of post transfusion complications. Therefore, the physico-chemical tests are performed on the infusion assemblies.

Physico-chemical tests :

Preparation of extract : Take three sets of infusion assembly, cut its PVC tubing and drip chamber into pieces of the size of 5 cm × 0.3 cm (maximum) to get total surface area of about 900 cm^2 ± 75 cm^2. Take these pieces into 500 ml beaker and rinse with 150 ml of distilled water for 30 sec., discard the liquid. Rinse again with distilled water. Transfer the prepared sample to a suitable extracting flask. Add 175 ml of distilled water. Take into another flask. Extract both the solution by heating in an oven at 70°C ± 1 °C for 24 hrs. Cool it, but not below 22 °C. Decant the extract immediately into another container and seal. Then the following tests are performed :

1. Appearance	Almost clear, colourless liquid.
2. pH	Between 3.5 and 7.0
3. Conductivity	75 micromho
4. Non-volatile residue	Not more than 15 mg. Evaporate 500 ml of extract. Wt. of empty dish and residue : ___ g. Wt. of empty dish : ___ g. Wt. of residue : ___ mg.
5. Pyrogen	Rabbit test as per I.P. Dose 10 ml/kg body weight of rabbit Limit : I.P.
6. Toxicity	As per I.P. Dose 0.5 ml/mice. Should be non-toxic as per I.P.
7. Sterility	As per I.P. Should be sterile as per I.P.

6. Syringes :

A syringe is a hollow, calibrated device which is intended to administer, accurate dosage of drugs into the human body via various routes of injections. These are made up glass or plastic materials.

Syringe are categorize into different criteria as mentioned below :

1. **On the basis of Capacity :**
   (a) Small syringe : Less than 10 ml.
   (b) Medium syringe : In between 10 - 100 ml.
   (c) Large syringe : 500 ml (For Enemata).

2. **On the basis of Application :**
   (a) Hypodermic syringes.
   (b) Bulb syringes.
   (c) Gravity syringes.

3. **On the basis of material used :**
   (a) Glass syringes : Are reusable.
   (b) Plastic syringes : Are disposable.

Plastic syringes are of two types :
1. Two-piece syringes
2. Three-piece syringes.

Let us understand the difference between 2-piece and 3-piece syringes.

2-piece syringe	**3-piece syringes**
It consists of two parts i.e. Barrel and Plunger.	It consists of three parts i.e. Barrel, plunger and a rubber gasket.

A diagram of 3-piece syringe of 5 ml capacity.

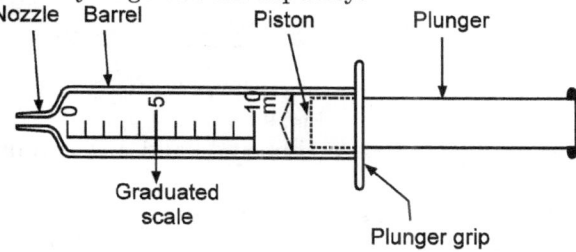

Fig. 9.7

7. Bulb syringes :

These syringes are used where sterility is not a concern and a fluid is to be administered in body cavities like nose, ear, vagina and rectum. These syringes have a value for wounds, infections, irritation and enema.

Fig. 9.8 : Ear syringe

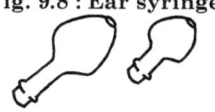

Fig. 9.9 : Nasal syringe

The nature of the bulb, length and tip of nozzle varies depending where it is used.

(a) Nasal syringes are of soft bulbs of about 10 ml capacity and the tip may be of glass or hard plastic.

(b) Ear syringe bulbs are soft, flexible rubber with long narrow nozzles.

(c) Rectal syringes bulbs have long and narrow nozzles and about 100 ml liquid can be administered enemata.

Rectal syringe :

Fig. 9.10

These are bulb type with long nozzle. Generally they are used for the enemata purpose in infants. The bulb is made up of rubber which has long two openings one connected to the reservoir and the other is connected to the spray tip. These are also known as valve syringes.

8. Needles :

There are two types of needles :
(a) Hypodermic needles.
(b) Surgical needles.

(a) Hypodermic needles : The term hypodermic is related with skin. It is derived from the words :
Hypo means : below or under.
Dermis means : skin.

(i) A needle is a thin, hallow tube attached to a plastic hub.

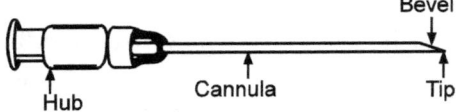

Fig. 9.11

(ii) A lumber puncture needle is used to withdraw CSF. It is about 10 cm long.

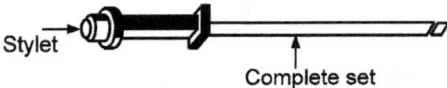

Fig. 9.12

(b) Surgical needles : These are thin and solid and are used for suturing and legating purposes.

They are in different sizes and shapes depending upon the application. They are of four types. The shaft may be flat, round, triangular and the tip is very sharp.

(i) Straight needle :

(ii) Flat shaft curved :

(iii) Round shaft curved :

(iv) Triangular shaft curved :

Fig. 9.13

Aneurysm needle is used for ligating. It has a handle for grip. The tip is blunt and curved with a hole.

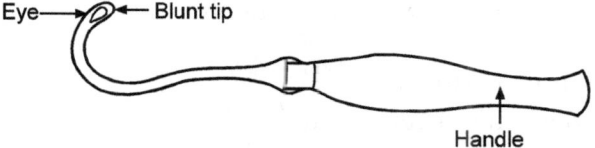

Fig. 9.14

Surgical sutures of ligatures :

Surgical ligature or suture is a thread or fibre specially prepared and sterilised for use in surgery. The thread used to tie blood vessels and tissue is called ligature, and the process is known as ligating. When the thread is used for sewing tissues together it is called suture.

Numerous types of materials have been used for the purpose including intestinal tissue, tendons, spun threads from vegetables, human and animal hairs, synthetic threads etc.

Properties of sutures :

1. They must be sterilize.
2. They must have an adequate strength.
3. They must have a gauge as fine as possible.
4. They must cause no irritation.
5. If absorbable their absorption time must be known.

Classification of Sutures :

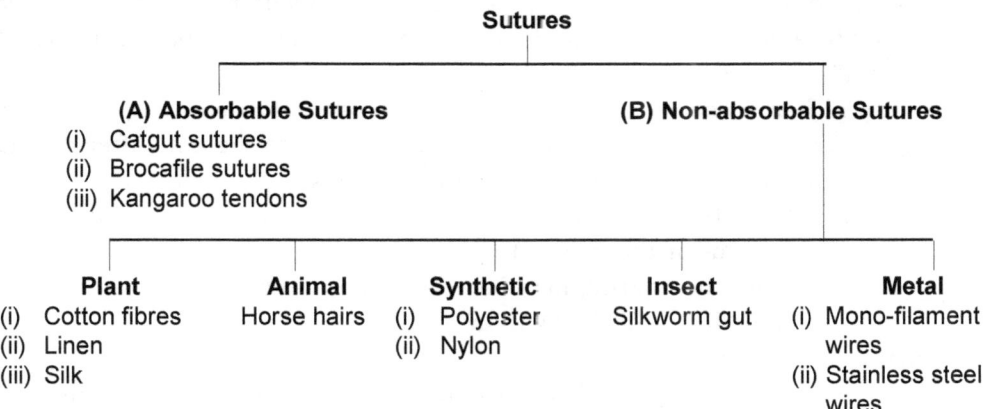

(A) Absorbable sutures :

Catgut suture : This is most widely used absorable suture and ligature material. Catgut or "violin" gut is prepared from intestine of the sheep. The name is derived from the greek word i.e. Kitgut.

Kit – means a small violin used in olden days.

Catgut is prepared from collagen of sheep purified and sterilised. The collagen is removed from the sub-mucous connective tissue of the intestinal part. After slaughtering the sheep about first 7 to 7.5 metre of intestine is selected. Then it is split into two ribbons, lengthwise. The sub-mucosal coat is removed by mechanical means and then the ribbons are spun into 5-6 threads. The atmospheric drying is done of the threads. Then the threads are treated with chromium salt solution to obtain a desired hardness to the strings. Finally polishing and gauging is done by mechanical process.

Sterilisation of catgut suture :

Absorbable sutures like catgut and kangaroo are sterilised by the following methods :

1. Chemical method :

In the beginning of the twentieth century iodine solution was used to a wide extent in Germany. This process needed much time and is a tedious one. The gut is immersed in a solution of iodine, but the disadvantage is that it requires long-time exposure which varies the absorption time of suture in the body.

Now-a-days *eto* sterilization technique is used worldwide. It is a very effective method because of the characteristic of ethylene oxide gas, which has penetration ability and wide spectrum of killing ability for microbes. This technique needs close monitoring otherwise it would alter the digestive properties of the gut.

2. By Heat method :

Catgut contains 15-25% of moisture. Heating above 80°C may cause hydrolysis resulting into formation of gelatin; therefore "Boilable and Non-boilable" methods are adopted. This comprises the following steps :

- **(a) Tubing :** A suitable length of gut is taken and coiled on a heat resistance fibre plate and then it is placed in a tube. The tube is labelled as "Heat resistant" by an ink.
- **(b) Drying :** Then these tubes are placed in a basket and dried in an oven. The temperature is raised slowly to prevent any damage to the gut. After drying it thoroughly, sterilization can be done by two ways :
  - (i) A basket of tube is placed in an autoclave containing an anhydrous fluid like xylene or toluene at 160°C for several hours.
  - (ii) Alternatively the heating may be done in non-pressure vessel at 160°C using high boiling anhydrous fluid.

3. Irradiation process :

In this method, the gut is packed in an aluminium foil packet containing IPA 90% as a preservative then the packet is passed through an irradiation area on a conveyor. Before opening the final pack, it is immersed in the solution of 1% formalin and 90% IPA.

Boilable and Non-boilable suture :

If any tubing fluid contains any water, the tube of the gut is labelled as "Non-boilable". This is a warning to avoid the use of heat is sterilizing the outside tube before opening it. These are more popular because the water keeps the gut pilable and immediately ready for use. The outside of the tube is sterilised by washing with soapy water and steeping in germicide solution before use.

If the tubing fluid is containing anhydrous fluid, and the tube may be boiled before opening then it is called "boilable" catgut.

QUESTIONS

1. Define surgical dressings / 'curatio'. **[S - 03]**
2. What is surgical guaze ? Give its uses. **[(S - 03, 96)]**
3. What are surgical dressings ? Give their uses. **[(S - 04, 02) 4 marks]**
4. Describe the four tests to evaluate absorbent cotton.   OR
   What are the tests for absorbent cotton according to it.
   [(S - 03, 02, 96) 4 marks]
5. Explain what is catheter. **[(S - 03) 4 marks]**
6. Explain what is Ryles tube and catheter. **[(S - 03) 4 marks]**
7. What is a B.T. set ? **[S - 04]**
8. What is I.V. set ? **[S - 04]**
9. What are the types of hypodermic syringes ? **[(W - 01) 4 marks]**
10. What is the use of rectal syringe ? **[S - 05]**
11. Define ligature and suture and classify them.
12. What is catgut or absorable suture ? How catgut suture is sterilised ?
13. What are boilable and non-boilable sutures ?

■■■

10

COMPUTERS

(The Versality)

INTRODUCTION

Presently computers have become a part of our lives and are used in a versatile manner in all walks of life e.g. hospitals, pharmacy, industries, banking, medical stores, pathology, teaching and learning, computer-based equipments, auto CAD, railway, airlines, graphics and for personal use.

Computer is an electronic machine which can accept data in a prescribed form, process it in a specified manner and supply the result in a predetermined form.

Computer system : There are three basic hardware components of a general purpose digital computer :
1. Central processing unit
2. Memory
3. Input/Output sections.

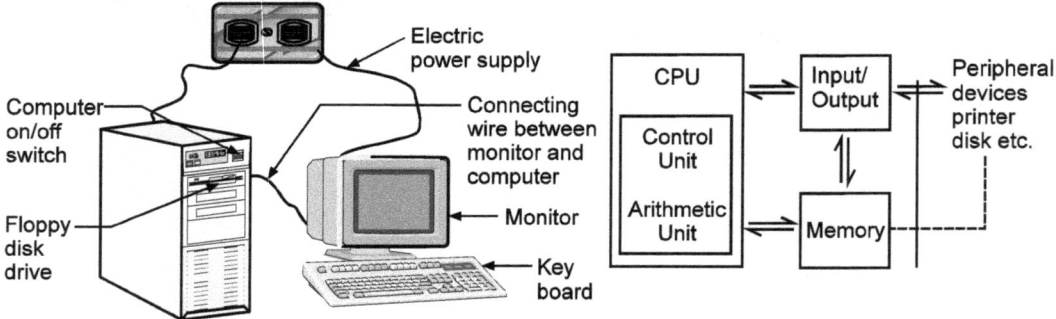

Fig. 10.1

1. **Central Processing Unit (CPU) :**
   CPU is the main unit of computer which acts like the brain of the human being. It carries all operations of the processes. It consists of three units.

   (a) Memory unit : It temporarily contains instructions, data and results.

   (b) Arithmetic and Logic Unit (ALU) : It performs operations like addition, subtraction, multiplication, division and comparison.

   (c) Central unit : It controls the transfer of data among different units.

2. **Monitor :**
   It is a display unit which shows the operational activities on a screen. There are two types : (a) monochrome, (b) colour.

3. **Hard Disk :**
   It is a storage device of the computer.

4. **Floppy Disk Drive :**
   It is used to back-up the data in a floppy.
5. **CD Drive / Pen Drive :**
   It can be used in a similar fashion as the floppy drive.
6. **Input Device :**
   Input device gives data in a readable form to the processing unit. The keyboard and the mouse are commonly used for this purpose.
7. **Output Device :**
   Printer is the best example of the output device from where the final print out is obtained. Three types of printers are available :
   (a) Dot matrix printer. (b) Graphics printer. (c) Laser printer.

Memory :
   It is a vital element of a computer system. The different memories are :
   1. Main memory (Primary memory)
   2. Mass memory (Secondary memory)
   1. Main Memory consists of :
      (a) **RAM** : It means Random Access Memory which helps in reading or writing for the unit.
      (b) **ROM** : Means Read only memory. A unit can only read information from this memory.

   Apart from this PROM (Programmable Read only memory) EPROM (Erasable PROM) MROM (Masked Read Only Memory) are also used in computers for different purposes.

Applications of Computers in Pharmacy :
   A major strength of the computers is that they can perform a wide range of operations. So, they could be utilised in pharmacy to save time and cost.

1. **Purchase and Inventory Control :**
   The computer has the ability to quickly calculate numerical data and compute statistical information. It plays an efficient role in the purchase and the inventory by maintaining the following information :

Drug code :	EOQ :
Description :	Re-order level :
Vendor :	Price :
Unit No/Size :	Issue :

2. **Drug store :**
   Different kinds of activities could be maintained as records like list of medicines, company details, order forms, billing and pricing, partly payment details, stock record etc. A drug list could be kept as productwise, categorywise or companywise.

3. **Drug distribution :**
   Entire drug distribution system could be followed up by maintaining, ward pharmacy record with charge floor stock system, non charge floor stock drugs record, individual patient order system etc.

4. **Hospital formulary :**
   It is advantageous to keep the formulary in computer because any up-date or amendment could be made easily without incurring any cost. Any one of the sections could be retrieved easily by putting a single command.

5. **Patient medical records :**
   Records like case paper and other records like test report, Diagnosis and treatment details which comprise History of the particular patient could be referred to easily within a few minutes.

6. **Drug Information Services :**
   It is an important tool for a pharmacist involved in drug information service. CD-ROM technique helps in the evolution of compact electronic libraries. Now-a-days CDs are available on different subjects etc.

7. **Patient monitoring :**
   Certain programmes have been designed to help in monitoring the patient with regard to diseases like, Asthama, CVD, diabetes etc. Such computers continuously record some physiological parameters.

8. **Community Pharmacy :**
   Educative programmes, on health education like, family welfare, AIDS and other communicable diseases could be communicated on web-sites through the internet facility.

Relevance of computer in information retrieval OR Information retrieval by computer

Computer have become an important necessity for pharmacist, who engaged in drug information services, patient counseling etc., so as to satisfy the queries related with medicine (such as actions of drugs, drug interaction, ADR, toxic effects etc.) or disease, disorder, acute syndrome, new innovative therapies etc. to the needy.

Since couple of years, this job of search has become easier by utilizing computers. A world known library, namely "National Library of medicine" have launched a computerized medical information system, known as Medical Literature Analysis Retrieval System (MEDLARS). Apart from this, the library also have developed a speed-up, working system, well known as MEDLINE.

By couple of years, CD-ROM technology has helped in the evaluation of compact electronic libraries. A private software company like Micro-medex provides for vast number of information on drugs.

Now-a-days, the academicians conducted demo pharmacology practicals on computer LAN system by using a single C.D. These C.Ds. are programmed by Ex-pharma (pharmatutor), a pioneer in this efforts.

Use of Computers in monitoring drugs to In-patients (hospitalized patients) :

For monitoring drug therapy in hospitalized patients, LAN computer terminals can be used by the pharmacist, either on each floor or at the patients bedside. This facility is made available which depends upon the size and the economical strength

of hospital. These terminals are operated under sophisticated programs for estimating drug levels and needed dosing parameters based on pharmacokinetic aspect. The monitoring of drugs comprises a cycle, that continues till the time of patient's hospitalization. The cycle includes :
  (i) Fill list of drugs, generated in the computer for ward patients.
  (ii) The pharmacist prepares and labels the drugs in accordance of the fill list.
  (iii) Prior to dispense those labelled unit dose for each patient, the pharmacist examine any possibility of drug interaction, such as drug-drug or drug-food. Then it sends to wards for administration to the patients.
  (iv) The entry of administered drugs is done in computer as medicine administration record.
  (v) Despite this diagnostic test drugs cost may be entered in the same.
  (vi) Lastly, at the time of discharge of the patient the above record is retrieved for final billing.

Use of Computers in purchase and inventory control of medicament

It is the major task for the hospital authorities to formulate an absolute inventory programme, which is essential to track the quantity of medicament available in drug store and processes order for it, when the medicament reaches to order point. This can be done by feeding different inventory techniques in computer program and are as :

1. **Utilization of perpetual inventory control :** The computer is linked with the operation such as receipt, issue, return and billing of goods; and hence at any time the stock position can be updated after every receipt and issue or returns.
2. **Setting of various levels :** The levels such as maximum level, minimum level, re-order quantity level and danger stock level. If these levels are feeded in computer program, it will help in tracking the optimum inventory, as well as prevent out of stock situation.
3. **Keeping the inventory records :** For accounting aspects, audit inspections and legal requirements, the records can be made ready at any time, by the use of computer through the above two inventory techniques.
4. **Measurement of inventory :** The price of each item can be feeded in computer to measure the value or those item for finding of total inventory of the hospital. The ABC technique of inventory can also be regulated by feeding their volume and cost.
5. **Finding of moving items :** This can be evaluate by analyzing its utilization from the stock record in computer at any framed frequencies in annum.
On the other hand this helps in assessing demand of any particular item.

QUESTION

1. Give the applications of computers in maintenance of records in hospitals/pharmacy. **[(S - 04, 02, 01, 97, 96 : W - 03, 00, 99) 4 marks]**

■■■

PART II : CLINICAL PHARMACY

1

INTRODUCTION TO CLINICAL PHARMACY

(The Pharmacy Practice)

INTRODUCTION

For the development of Clinical Pharmacy as a new aspect one should have knowledge for effective use of drug, about its uses and adverse effects, drug interaction and safe medication.

Clinical pharmacy is a branch of pharmaceutical science which deals with various aspects of patient care, not only with dispensing of drugs, but advising the patient on rational selection and safe use of drug.

Scope of Clinical Pharmacy :

1. **Evaluation and Selection of drugs :**

   Therapeutic equivalency of different dosage form is evaluated by using biopharmaceutics. It can give unique services in the selection of drug.

2. **Drug Information :**

   The field realises the importance of keeping information, use of information retrieval techniques to make any data available in an efficient manner. The Drug Information centre acts as a data bank.

3. **Drug utilisation :**

   Clinical pharmacy helps in the study of drug abuse, drug misuse, medication error etc. So as to overcome such abrupt, rational and safe use of medicine.

4. **Education and Training Programmes :**

   A Role has been played in educating medical and para-medical staff on rational drug therapy.

5. **Patient care :**

   It is a prime duty of clinical pharmacy area to monitor the drug therapy.

Objectives of Clinical Pharmacy :

The scenario of clinical pharmacy practices have been significantly changed, with respect of the emergence and explosive increase in the availability of thousands of drugs and the tremendous load on the physician, compel him to depend upon the pharmacist for imparting drug and therapy related information exclusively to the in-patient. The pharmacist may bridge the gap between the physician and the patient by virtue of the objectives of clinical pharmacy and those are as below :

(i) It provides the platform to the fellow students to interact with the physician to obtain better understanding of prescribed medicine.
(ii) It gives opportunity to assist the physician in doing a better job of prescribing and observing drug therapy.
(iii) It also offers an opportunity to educate the patients by involving them in the process of drug utilization.
(iv) It creates opportunities of clinical oriented research and development, such as clinical trials, therapeutic drug monitoring etc.

Health Care Team :

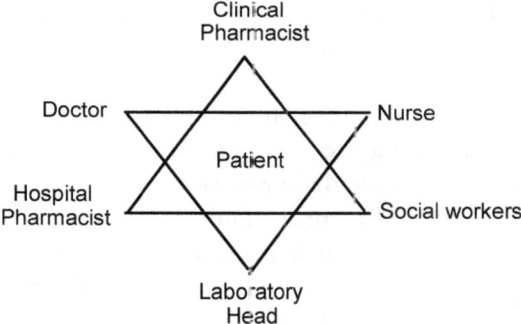

Medication History :

Medication history means a patient's record. Each and every patient's record is maintained in a big hospital. This exercise has become more easier due to availability of computers. The community should be advised to keep medication history right from the beginning of the birth of child.

A history consists of the following information of the patient.
- Name
- Gender
- Date of birth
- Blood group –   Rh factor
- Immunization schedule
- Booster dose dates
- Therapy details given for the diseases.
- Heriditary disease details

- ADR details
- Self-medication
- Periodically affected by any disease
- Habits, like drinks, tobacco, smoking etc.
- Drug withdrawal symptoms if any.

Significance of medication history :
1. It can be used as a gauze by the physician for therapy.
2. Patient compliance for drug can be studied.
3. A reason for ADR or allergy can be understood.
4. Patients routine life pattern could be studied.
5. To know the patients current and past medications.
6. Counselling become easier after knowing all details to the pharmacist.

Role of Clinical Pharmacist :
1. He prepares the case history of the patient, which includes current sign and symptoms and past history.
2. He assists the physician and the patient in getting diagnostic tests.
3. He delivers options on selecting drugs and dosage forms to the physician for therapy to be followed.
4. Patient counselling and advices during his ward visit.
5. Patient's Drug monitoring during his stay in the hospital.
6. Detects and reports adverse drug reactions.
7. Keeps prescription profile records of out-patients.
8. Participates in quality assurance programs and clinical drug investigations.
9. Monitors patients compliance during his stay in the hospital.
10. Assumes care and responsibility for drug regulatory affairs.

A diagrammatic Summary of Role of Clinical Pharmacist

Fig. 1.1

QUESTIONS

1. Define clinical pharmacy. **[W - 9]**
2. What is clinical pharmacy ? **[S - 97, 01 : W - 02, 00]**
3. What is the significance of patient medication history ? **[W - 03]**
4. Discuss the role of clinical pharmacist. **[W - 01]**

■■■

2. MODERN DISPENSING ASPECTS

(The Concept of Global Pharmacy)

INTRODUCTION

Since long, prescription has been the only link between the physician, the pharmacist and the patient. Following the prescription and dispensing of medicine, it is expected that the patient will follow the instructions by the label.

But in India a major population is living in rural and urban areas. According to NCPIE's (National Council of Patient Information and Education) survey, the reasons of non-adherence to the instructions are summarised as :

Sr. No.	Reasons of Non Adherence	% Population
1.	Busy Schedule of work	52
2.	Away from home	46
3.	Change in daily routine	45
4.	Negligence	20
5.	Hesitation	17
6.	Confusion about directions of dosage	14

Success of drug therapy mainly depends on adherence or compliance. Illiteracy and lack of knowledge comprises non or poor compliance. To improve this, patient education is must. The pharmacists play a vital role in guiding the patients on prescribed drugs and counselling them about proper and safe use of medicines.

Patient Counselling :

Patient counselling can be defined as providing medication information orally, in written or by showing pictograms to the patients or their relatives on directions of use, precautions, storage and diet etc.

Location for counselling centre :

The ideal location for the **counselling centre** may be near to the "OPD Dispensary" as the hospital pharmacy, in very big hospitals, runs round the clock in shifts. Most of the OPD prescriptions come to the main pharmacy and it may handle nearly, more than thousand per day; thereby most of the patients will be benefited.

The materials used for patient counselling are categorised into the following groups :

1. **Library sources :**
   - Text books
   - Reference books

- CIMS
- IDR
- ASHP guidelines

2. **Counselling AIDs :**
   - Inhalers
   - Nebulizers
   - Sprays

3. **Use of pictograms :**

Do not store medicine where children can reach.

Fig. 2.1 : Do not store medicine where children can reach

Prior to counselling the patients, a pharmacist must know the past history related to diseases like Diabetes, hypertension, liver or renal impairment etc. or allergic reactions to drug taken previously.

The counselling information a pharmacist can deliver with an appropriate meaning and simple language is summarised as :

(A) On Administration of Drug :
- Do not take on empty stomach or with milk/food.
- Do not swallow the tablet or chew it (e.g. Lozenges)
- Shake well before use in case of liquids.
- Dosage schedule to be taken per day.
- Do not use the lid of bottle to take the liquid medicine.

(B) On proper and safe use of medicine :
- Proper direction for use of the drug should be given e.g. in case of eye-drop; how to apply the dropper on container and instill the solution.
- Duration of course for which drug has to be taken.
- Do not go for concurrent administration of drugs prescribed at a schedule time dose.

(C) On storage of medicines :
- Store it in a dry, cool and dark place.
- Expired medicine should be discarded.
- Close the lid on the bottle properly.
- Keep the medicine away from the reach of children.

Advantages / Significance's of patient counselling :

1. **Ensures :** Safe use and proper storage of medicine.

2. **Medication Errors :** are minimised because of general advices given to the patients on prescribed drugs.
3. **Education :** The health community can be educated on epidemics, endemic and health education etc.
4. **Awareness :** It is essential to mention the role of the pharmacist and the services rendered by the pharmacy to the society.
5. **Success of therapy :** Adequate information delivered by the pharmacist, during his ward visit, hastens the well being of the patient.
6. **Prestige and Image :** The services given on advices and patient counselling to the health community helps in building of prestige and image of the hospital.

General advice on prescribed drugs : To ensure adequate compliance and adherence for success of the drug therapy, a pharmacist should render proper advice. Some of them are as under :

- **Antacid tablet :** Do not swallow the tablet. Chew and masticate till it dissolves in the mouth.
- **Ampicillin :** Take it at a scheduled time, even you skip the meal. It should be taken on empty stomach atleast 1 hr. before or 2-3 hrs after meal.
- **Boric acid :** Do not take it orally. Keep it away from the reach of children below 12 years old.
- **Castor oil and liquid paraffin :** Do not consume it for prolonged time and take it at bed time only.
- **Diazepam :** Drug produces drowsiness, therefore do not drive a vehicle or work on dangerous machines.
- **Haematinics :** Take after meal and if constipation results, consult the physician.
- **Oxyphenbutazone :** Do not take on empty stomach.
- **Phenolpthalein :** It may colour the urine and faeces pink, hence do not consult the doctor.
- **Rifampicin :** Take it on empty stomach. It may change the colour of urine to red; so no need to contact the doctor.
- **Sulpha drugs :** Take with plenty of milk or water and drink maximum water during day time.
- **Salicytates :** Do not take this drug on empty stomach. Take it with milk or water.
- **Vaginal contraceptive suppositories :** Insert the suppositories about 30 min. before conception and keep atleast 6 hrs. in the vigina.
- **Tetracyline and Bisacodyl :** Do not take with milk, antacids or food containing calcium.
- **Antihistaminics :** It may cause sedation so do not worry about it.

- **Antidiabetics and Metronidazole :** Avoid alcoholic beverages.
- **MAO inhibitors :** Avoid food containing cheese, butter and alcohol beverages.
- **Nitrates :** Potent medican do not stop medication without consultation with physician.
- **Phenytoin :** Expose yourself to sunlight in the morning.

Patient Compliance :

Despite the efforts of pharmacists and other health care parameters, medication non-adherence remains a major public health problem. Non-compliance with the therapeutic region can produce a dangerous situation which may result in re-hospitalisation e.g. in case of psychiatric patients, chemotherapy of T.B., Cancer etc.

Compliance can be calculated by the equation :

$$\text{Patient compliance} = \frac{NPD - NMD}{NPD} \times 100$$

NPD : No. of patients prescribed dosage
NMD : No. of medication errors

Compliance is defined as faithful adherence by the patient to the instructions of prescriber. It can be categorised on the basis of degree of compliance.

(a) **Total compliance :** A patient adheres to the instructions of a physician in a ratio of 85-100% on a given prescription.

(b) **Partial compliance :** It is a situation, where the patient frequently forgets to take medicine as per the given directions.

(c) **Non-compliance :** The medicine is taken by the patient in a very irregular manner, in a range of 0 - 50%.

(d) **Interval (Timing) non-compliance :** Prescribed schedule dosages of medicine are not taken at regular timing. e.g. If a drug is to be taken at every 6 hrs; it can be interpreted as 4 times in 24 hrs. **or** 3 times in working hrs (i.e. 18 hrs).

(e) **Over-compliance :** A condition where the dosage or quantity of drug is taken more than prescribed; may result into adverse effect.

Non-compliance is the main trouble of the health community. It can be expressed as a number of dosage not taken or taken incorrectly that alters the patient's therapeutic response.

Types of Non-Compliance :

The types are on the basis of happenings :

(i) **Error non-compliance :** In taking dosages of drugs.
(ii) **Omission non-compliance :** Some dosages of drugs are omitted.
(iii) **Failure non-compliance :** Patient fails to obtain medicine.
(iv) **Discontinuation non-compliance :** Patient stopped medication without consulting his physician.

Reasons for Non-Compliance :
- **(i) Multiple drug therapy :** Due to greater number of drugs taken by the patient there is possibility of risk of non-compliance. Similarity of shape, size or colour of drugs causes confusion.
- **(ii) Frequency of administration :** Regular schedule of dosage regime cannot be followed due to work load.
- **(iii) Period of therapy :** The chances of non-compliance is greater because of longer duration of treatment in cases of chronic diseases.
- **(iv) Side effects :** There is hindrance of taking medicine due to nausea and vomiting or GI upset may cause non-compliance.
- **(v) Cost of medication :** Specially poor class patients are suffering. It is an important aspect affecting compliance.

Consequences of Non-Compliance :

On clinical ground, it is essential to follow the instructions given by the physician for the success of therapy. If these instructions violate at the patient level, that results into following consequences of non-compliance :

- **(i) Drug tolerance :** It may develop on discontinuation therapy or irregular administration of drugs, such as antibiotics, anti-psychotics and chemotherapeutic agents.
- **(ii) Drug abuse or addiction :** It results due to repeated consumption of OTC drugs like cough preparation, laxatives or anxiolytics etc.
- **(iii) Adverse reactions :** Such reactions may occur due over consumption or repeated administration of potent drugs, like hypertensive, anti-diabetic or steroids etc.
- **(iv) Potential risk :** Chances of potential risk arise from sudden stoppage of chronic treatment with anti-tuberculuar drugs, anti-convulscent etc.
- **(v) Recurrence of infection :** If the patient consumes less quantity of drugs, thereby depriving the patient of the full therapeutic effect and possibility of a progressive worsening of his condition or recurrence of infection such as malaria, thyphoid etc.

Medication Errors :

The past couple of years have been characterised by significant changes in dispensing of drugs. The way we work, communicate, counsel, conduct research and implement adequate regulatory measures to safeguard the public health.

A medication error is a preventable event that occurs in the process of medication at any stage like prescribing, dispensing and administration of drug.

In USA, there are reports of medication errors and was studied by giving a dose error at an interval of every six doses of medication in unit dose dispensing.

Reasons of medication errors :
- (i) Wrong interpretation of prescription.
- (ii) Wrong doses due to mis-calculations.

(iii) Inadequate labelling information for patient.
(iv) No knowledge of proper drug compliance.
(v) Environment factors such as light, noise and interruptions may split concentration of pharmacist.

Kinds of medication errors :
1. **Prescribing errors :** It may result due to insufficient information about the patients medical history. The doctor may commit the error in writing prescription.
2. **Dispensing error :** Mis-interpretation and mis-perception due to insufficient information in prescription may result in the wrong calculations of doses especially among childrens.
3. **Drug administration error :** It occurs due to wrong route of administration, wrong dose administration or even the drug being given to wrong patients.

Outcome of medication error :
The outcome may be serious, resulting in the following :
(i) Adverse Drug Reactions (ADR)
(ii) Drug-Drug interactions (DDI)
(iii) Drug Related Morbidity (DRM).

QUESTIONS

1. What is patient compliance ? **[(W - 00, 01) 4 marks]**
2. What are the advantages or significances of patient counselling ?
   [(W - 03, 01, 00, 97) 4 marks]
3. Write a note on patient compliance. **[S - 03]**
4. What advice must be given to the patient while prescribing the following drugs.
   (i) Boric acid
   (ii) Salicylates
   (iii) Ampicillin
   (iv) Phendphthalein
   (v) Antacid tablet
   (vi) Haematinics
   (vii) Phenytoin
   (viii) Castor oil
   (ix) Vaginal contraceptive suppositories.
   [(S - 04, 02, 99, 97, 96 : W - 03, 00, 99) 1 mark each]

■■■

3
MEDICAL TERMINOLOGY

INTRODUCTION

At present, the job of compounding has largely been taken over by the industry. The present day pharmacist diverts more to patient-oriented services. The role of the pharmacist in counselling and health education has been appreciated.

A general physician would expect to take care of dosage requirements and adjust dosage form and helps the patient to understand how to take or apply them.

Hence the pharmacist should know the medical and routine terminology including latin terms and weight/measures.

(A) List of commonly used dosage forms :

Sr. No.		Dosage Form	Definition
(a)	Liquids		
1.		Solution	Solution is a liquid preparation that contains one or more soluble substances dissolved in a specific solvent.
2.		Draughts	It is a simple solution containing a single dose in a separate bottle.
3.		Drop	It is generally for vitamins and antibiotics formulation for paediatric purpose.
4.		Linctus	Linctus is a cough preparation, containing expectorants in a vehicle of simple syrup.
5.		Syrups	Syrups are concentrated aqueous solutions of sucrose or other sugar. They may be viscous in nature and sweet in taste.
6.		Elixirs	Elixirs are clear, flavoured and sweetened hydro-alcoholic liquids.
7.		Mixture	It is a liquid medicine for oral use of which several dosages are contained in aqueous form.

(3.1)

8.		Tincture	Tinctures are alcoholic or aqueous extracts obtained from botanical parts of a medical plant.
9.		Emulsions	Are heterogeneous liquid dosage forms in which a immiscible liquid is dispersed with the help of emulsifying agent in a continuous phase.
10.		Suspension	A coarse dispersion containing finely divided insoluble material suspended in liquid medium.
11.		Liniments	Are liquids or viscous preparations intended for external use.
12.		Lotions	Lotions are alcoholic or aqueous liquids intended for external application.
13.		Enemas	Enemas are aqueous or oily solutions administered in rectum to cause evacuation.
(b)	Semi-solids	Ointment	Ointments are soft, semisolid greasy preparations intended for application to skin with or without rubbing.
1.		Creams	Cream is a viscous emulsion of semi-solid consistency intended for external application.
2.		Pastes	Pastes are ointment like preparations for external use, containing high percentage of insoluble solids.
3.		Poultices	Poultices are soft, viscous and pasty preparations applied to skin when they are hot.
(c)	Solids	Powders	Are homogenous mixture of drugs and chemicals in a dry and fine state.
1.		Snaff	These are powders which are insufflated in nasal cavity.
2.		Capsules	A medicament(s) enclosed in a shell of gelatin.
3.		Tablet	Tablet is a form containing a medicament(s) with or without pharmaceutical aids, prepared by compression.
4.		Pills	Pills are small, round or egg shaped bodies for oral administration.

(B) Common Pharmacological terms :

Sr. No.	Dosage Form	Definition	Examples
1.	Analeptics	Drugs that stimulate CNS and respiration.	Caffeine, Aromatics
2.	Anaesthetics	Are drugs that produce anaesthesia, abolished sensation of pain.	Thiopental propofol.
3.	Antacids	Drugs that normalise the hyper secretion of acid in stomach.	$Al(OH)_3$ gel Na-bicarbonate
4.	Astringents	Drugs that cause precipitation of proteins.	Tannic acid.
5.	Carminatives	Drugs which expel the gas from G.I.T.	Tr. Cardamom Aromatic waters
6.	Chemotherapy	Drugs that kill micro-organisms and pathogens multiplying in host cell with chemotherapeutic agent.	Rifampicin streptomycin
7.	Cholagogues	Drugs help in evacuation of the gall bladder	Ipecac, calomel
8.	Diuretics	Drug which increases excretion of water and electrolyte with flow of urine	Theophylline Thiomersals
9.	Emetics	Drugs which induce emesis	Bitters, Ipecac
10.	Haematinics	Drugs which increase the formation of blood and haemoglobin	Iron, ferrous-gluconate
11.	Purgatives	Drugs that promote the evacuation of bowels	Senna, castor oil
12.	Tranquilizers	Drugs that reduce anxiety and produce sedation	Diazepam Lorazepam

(C) Appropriate meanings of terms :

Sr. No.	Term	Meaning
1.	Etiology	Cause of disease.
2.	Disease	Physiological modifications or resulting of abnormal functioning of organ or organ system.
3.	Arthritis	Inflammation of joints.
4.	Myalgia	Pain of skeletal muscle
5.	Osteosporesis	Degenerative condition of bones.
6.	Ischemia	Reduction of blood supply to heart.
7.	Arthythmia	Disturbances in the normal cardiac rhythm.
8.	Tachycardia	Increase in heart beat rate.
9.	Bradycardia	Decrease in heart beat rate.
10.	Pyrexia	Increase in body temperature (fever)
11.	Meningitis	Inflammation to the covering of brains.
12.	Insomnia	State of chronic sleeplessness.
13.	Coma	Deep sleep with complete loss of consciousness.
14.	Miosis	Contraction of pupil.
15.	Mydriasis	Dilation of pupil.
16.	Apnoea	Temporary cessation of respiration.
17.	Dysponea	Difficulty in breathing.
18.	Anoxia	Lack of oxygen in tissue.
19.	Anorexia	Loss of appetite.
20.	Dyspepsia	State of Indigestion.
21.	Dysphagia	Difficulty in swallowing.
22.	Flatulence	Formation of gas in the digestive tract.
23.	Necrosis	Death of tissue in localised area.
24.	Immunity	Resistance of a body to invading microbes.
25.	Lesion	It is a outcome in the form of injury/wounds in the body due to disease.

(D) Latin Terms and Phase :

Sr. No.	Terms	Abbreviation	Meaning
1.	**Prepositions :**		
	Ana	aa	of each
	Ante	a	Before
	Post	p	After
	Secundum	—	According to

2.	**Dosage Forms :**		
	Tussin		
	Auristillae	auri still.	The ear drop
	Cataplasma	Cataplasm	A poultice
	Charata	Chart	A powder
	Collutorium		
	Emulsio	Emul.	An emulsion
	Enema	–	An Enema
	Guttae	gtt.	Drop
	Haustus	ht.	Draught (A single dose mixture)
	Lotio	lot.	A lotion
	Mistura	m. mist	A mixture
	Nebula	neb.	A spray solution
	Pasta	past.	A paste
	Pulvis	pulv.	A powder
	Unguentum	Ung.	An ointment
3.	**Administration OR Application**		
	Addendus	Addend.	To be added
	Capiendus	Capiend	To be taken
	Dandus	Dand	To be given
	More dicto	M.d.	As directed
	Sumendus	S. Sum.	To be taken
	Utendus	U. Utend.	To be used
4.	**Timing :**		
	SOS	p.r.m. (proreneta)	Occasionally when required.
	Semel die	Sem. die	Once a day
	Bis in die	b.i.d.	Twice a day
	Ter in die	T.i.d.	Thrice a day
	Mane	m.	In the morning
	Vespere	vesp.	In the evening
	Nocte	n.	At night
	Omni nocte	o.m.	Every night
	Ante cibos	a.c.	Before meal
	Post cibos	p.c.	After meal
	Hora Somni	h. somni.	At bed time.

5.	Miscellaneous		
	Fortis	–	Strong
	Dura	–	Hard
	Ameri	–	Bitter
	Dalcis	–	Sweet
	Semel	–	Once
	Simul	–	Together
	Folium	–	Leaf

(E) Latin terms of weight and measures

Sr. No.	Latin	Abbreviation	Meaning	Symbol
1.	Congius	cong.	Gallon	C
2.	Drachma	dr.	drachm	3
3.	Fluid drachma	fl. dr.	fluid drachm	fl. 3
4.	Fluid unica	fl. unc.	fluid ounce	oz
5.	Granum	gr.	grain	gr
6.	Libra	libr.	pound	lb
7.	Minimum	m.	minim	m
8.	Uncia	oz	ounce	oz

(F) List of common abbreviations and meaning :

Term	Meaning
Hb	Haemoglobin
RBC	Red Blood Cells
PCV	Packed Cell Volume
MCV	Mean Corpuscular Volume
MCH	Mean Corpuscular Haemoglobin
MCHC	Mean Corpuscular Haemoglobin concentration
ESR	Erythrocyte Sedimentation Rate
BP	Blood Pressure
PP	Pulse Pressure
WBC	White Blood Cells

DLC	Differential Leucocyte Count	
BBB	Blood Brain Barrier	
BMR	Basal Metabolic Rate	
BBT	Basal Body Temperature	
BUN	Blood Nitrogen Urea	
HDL	High Density Lipoprotein	
LDL	Low Density Lipoprotein	
LDH	Lactic Acid Dehydrogenase	
SGPT	Serum Glutamic Pyruvic Transaminase	
SGOT	Serum Glutamic Oxalacetic Transaminase	
AST	Aspirate Transaminase	
ALP	Alkaline Phosphatase	
ALT	Alanine Transaminase	

(G) List of diseases with meaning :

Disease	Meaning
Addisons disease	Hyposecretion of adrenal cortex.
Adinoids	Enlargement of pharyngeal tonsils.
Bell's palsy	Compression of facial nerve.
Buerger's disease	Inflammation with thrombosis in small arteries.
Conn's syndrome	An excessive secretion of minerolocorticoids.
Crohn's disease	Inflammatory condition of G.I.T.
Crush syndrome	Sustained pressure on muscle, causes necrosis.
Cushings syndrome	Hyper secretion of adrenal cortex.
Grave's disease	It is a thyrotoxicosis.
Hodgkin's disease	Enlargement of lymph node.
Icterus	It is a form of jaundice.
Lorain-Levi syndrome	Severe deficiency of growth hormone.
Menier's disease	Pressure increases in membranous labyrinth.
Simmond's disease (Sheehan's syndrome)	It is a penhypo-pituitarism in adults.

(H) Other terms :

(i) Immunity	It is a natural resistance body mechanism against the invasion of micro-organism which causes disease or infection.
(ii) Susceptibility	It is a state arises in the body by virtue of it an individual prones to happen a infection.
(iii) Superinfection	It is an infection which progresses during existing any kind of infection. e.g. During T.B. pneumonia develops.
(iv) Contraindications	It means drug or medicine is prohibited to administered under particular circumstances or situations.

QUESTIONS

1. Define the terms any five : Snuff, Poultice, Tinctures, Emulsions, Suppositories, Tablets, Syrups. **[(S - 04, 02, 01) 5 marks]**

2. Give the meaning of following :

   Necrosis, Coma, Insomnia, Anorexia, Dysponea, Arrythmia, Amnesia, Flatulence, Osteoporesis, Emetics, Analeptics, Astringents, Etioilogy, Lesion.

   [(S - 04, 03, 99, 97, 96 : W - 03, 02, 01, 00) 5 marks]

3. Translate into English :

   Semel, Ana, Nebula, Folium, Unus, Mane.

   [(S - 04, 01, 97, 96 : W - 02, 00) 5 marks]

■■■

4

DISEASES, MANIFESTATIONS AND SYMPTOMS

INTRODUCTION

Disease : It is a state of alteration in normal physiological functioning with physical or mental discomfort caused due to modifications taken place in the body or invasion of micro-organisms or toxic effect produced by any chemical substance.

Manifestations : The numerous changes observed or perceived in the body due to the disease condition.

They could be demonstrated by using the following terms :

1. **Signs :** Signs of disease are observable ones objectively, viz. fever, swelling, shivering and redness of skin etc.

2. **Symptoms :** Symptoms cannot be observed by others, but felt by himself like pain, uneasiness, nausea burning sensations, irritation, dryness of mouth etc.

3. **Lesion :** Injury or wounds resulted in the body structure due to disease.

4. **Sequel :** The outcome of a disease is referred in some cases as a sequel. e.g. jaundice after malerial infection, scar left after curing of wound.

The disesase can be categorised as :

(a) **Infectious diseases :** e.g. Tuberculosis, pneumonia etc.

(b) **Serological diseases :** e.g. Hepatitis, AIDS.

(c) **Autoimmune disease :** e.g. Rheumatoid arthritis.

(d) **Endocrine / Exocrine disorders :** Diabetes, peptic ulcer.

(e) **Congenital or Acquired disorders :** Cardiovascular diseases.

(f) **Functional disease :** Epilepsy.

1. TUBERCULOSIS

Tuberculosis is a communicable, chronic disease caused by Mycobacterium tuberculosis and M-bovis. It is studied by the scientist, namely, Robert Koch. Few decades before, tuberculosis is referred as "King of diseases".

Epidemology : It is estimated that 1.7 billion individuals are infected world wide, with 8 - 10 million new cases and 3 million deaths per year. WHO estimates the tuberculosis cases 6% of all deaths worldwide. It is found that HIV infected persons are prone to active tuberculosis.

Pathophysiology : Mycobacterium tuberculosis are slender, rod shape, aerobic bacteria; infected to the host by air born contamination. It affects firstly the lungs due to its oxygen rich environment. These bacilli well-multiply and grow in the oxygen-rich lungs. As the gravity of the disease increases, organs like bones, liver, lymph, tissue etc. get affected. Hence, it comprises pulmonary and extra-pulmonary tuberculosis respectively. The tuberculosis consists of :

(a) **Primary pulmonary tuberculosis :** With primary T.B., the source of organism is exogeneous. It occurs in individuals, who may lose their sensitivity for autoimmune systems of body to tubercule bacillus. And so may develop primary tuberculosis more than once.

(b) **Secondary pulmonary tuberculosis :** It is also called "Reactive tuberculosis". It may follow shortly after primary pulmonary tuberculosis in which the resistance of the body is decreased markedly. It is an exogenous re-infection. It is mainly found in the apex of one or both the upper lobes of lungs.

(c) **Miliary Tuberculosis :** It is an extra-pulmonary form, which results from progressive primary T.B. as well secondary T.B. This is a lymphohaematogenous disease which spreads in later stages into systemic organs or isolated organs as liver, brain, kidney, in pulmonary artery, lymph nodes and bone cells etc.

Signs and Symptoms :

(i) Pyrexia - normally rise in body temperature in evening.

(ii) Fatigue, malaise and loss in body weight.

(iii) Loss of appetite, night sweats.

(iv) Prolonged cough with green and yellow sputum and pain in the chest.

(v) Blood stains persist in sputum due to inflammation of pleura or pericardium (ulcerative condition).

(vi) Pulmonary artery in tubercle region breaks, which results into massive haemorrhage.

Treatment :

The treatment of tuberculosis initiated with multiple drug therapy followed in following manner :

1. Use of first line drugs : Combination of these drugs, such as Rifampin, Isoniazid, Pyrizinamide, Streptomycin and Ethambutol. The combination of these drugs have a greatest efficacy and an acceptable level of toxicity and it is adopted in the following fashion.

(a) A treatment starts with ...

Rifampin + Isoniazide + Pyrizinamide + Ethambutol for period of first 2 to 3 months.

The reason of using Ethambutol with the combination is to prevent the primary resistance to isoniazide.

(b) Then it followed with ...

Rifampin + Isoniazid + Ethambutol

(c) Supportive measures ...

Vitamin B_6 is given orally during therapy to nulify toxic effect that is neuritis. High protein diet is recommended like serals, meat, eggs, milk etc. to gain the body weight.

2. Use of second line drugs : In case of re-occurrence or resistance develops to first line drugs then these drugs such as Ethionamide, Cycloserine, aminosalicylic acid are used.

2. HEPATITIS

Hepatitis is an infectious viral, inflammatory disorder caused due to various factors, such as drug toxicity, alcoholic diseases and autoimmune. There are different types of hepatitis.

Epidemology :

1. **Hepatitis A (HAV) :** It is also known as infectious hepatitis HAV spreads by ingestion of contaminated water, food and after jaundice. It is a small non-enveloped, single strand RNA picorna-virus. The virus itself does not appear to be cytotoxic to hepatocytes. The injury results from autoimmune mediated damage.

2. **Hepatitis B (HBV) :** It is also known as serological hepatitis.

    It is :

    (a) Acute hepatitis

    (b) Chronic hepatitis and

    (c) Progressive hepatitis disease.

Ending in cirrhosis. This is transmitted through contaminated syringes and needles, blood transfusion and tattooing etc.

It is DNA containing virus. The genome of HBV is partially double-strand circular DNA. This virus is replicated in liver but does not act as hepatotoxic.

3. **Hepatitis C (HCV)** : It is a major cause of liver diseases worldwide. The routes of transmission are blood transfusion, contaminated needles and sexual contact. It is heterogenous group of RNA-depended virus having small, enveloped single strand.

4. **Hepatitis D (HDV)** : This is also known as Delta hepatitis. This virus can replicate only in the presence of the helper B virus.

5. **Hepatitis E (HEV)** : This is a water borne infection occuring primarily in young to middle age adults. HEV is an enveloped single-strand RNA virus. It can be detected in stool.

6. **Hepatitis G (HGV)** : Epidemiologic studies have established that some cases of hepatitis are caused by infectious agent designed as "F" and "G".

Pathophysiology :

Heptatitis A virus is relatively heat resistant. Once the virus enters the body, it multiplies in the intestinal epithelial mucosa and escapes into the liver by the circulatory system. HBV replicates in the liver cells and its fragments get incorporated in the liver cell membranes and the manifestations are because of immune response to the infection.

The incubation period of HAV is about 2-6 weeks developed in two stages that are prodromal or pre-icteric and icteric. HBV need 3 to 6 months for incubation.

Signs and Symptoms : The signs and symptoms are almost similar in all the types, but usually more severe in case of HBV and HCV. These are as under :

(i) Uneasiness, nausea vomitting with fever.
(ii) Loss of appetite and body weight.
(iii) Intolerance to fatty food due to tenderness of liver.
(iv) Changes in smell, taste and sense with pharyngitis and cough.
(v) Urine darkens due to rise in bilirubin serum level to about 2 mg/100 ml (Normal 0.3 to 1.1 mg/100 ml) and it reaches to a stage of jaundice.

Once the condition reaches to jaundice, the clinical features are identical in all the types of hepatitis :

(i) The GIT symptoms decreases with severity of the disease.
(ii) SGOT and SGPT levels are increased prior to onset of jaundice.
(iii) Necrosis of hepatocytes with altered cell permeability.
(iv) Globulin level is commonly increased.
(v) Serum bilirubin level may increases to 2 to 20 mg/100 ml.

Treatment :

Treatment of hepatitis includes :

1. **Monotherapy :**
   - Interferon alfa - 2A : 2.5 - 5 mu 3 times/week for 4-6 months.
   - Penicillamine - Initially 500 mg in divided doses.
   - Interferon alfa - 2B : 5 mu by IM/SC daily for 16 weeks.

2. **Combination therapy :**
   - Ribavirin + Interferon Alfa - 2B.
   - Lamivudine + Zodovudine

3. **Hepato-protectives :** Silymarin - 140 mg b.i.d./t.i.d.

3. RHEUMATOID ARTHRITIS

Rheumatoid Arthritis (RA) is a systemic, chronic, autoimmune, inflammatory disease that affects mainly the joints and sometimes other organs and tissues.

Pathophysiology :

This is an immunological, medicated disease characterised by inflammation of joints due to the following factors :

(i) Activation of macrophages and other cells in the joint space due to appearance of "RA factor - IgG" complex in joints. This releases lysozomal enzymes which break-down collagen fibres and damage the articular cartilage. Once the cartilages of bone joints are damaged, it results into inflammation with pain of joints.

(ii) Activation of β-cells system, produces antibodies. Mainly immunoglobulin M and G variety called "IgM" and "IgG" respectively in presence of RA factor. The resultant autoimmune reactions damage the structure of joint, which plays a role in the progress of the disease.

Signs and Symptoms :

(i) Weakness with loss of appetite and body weight.

(ii) Malaise and low grade fever.

(iii) Inflammation of the joints with aching and stiffness particularly in the morning.

(iv) As the disease progresses, enlargement of joints and restricted movement occurs.

(v) Joints of finger may become immobilised.

(vi) Anaemia may occur in chronic conditions.

(vii) Appearance of Raynaud's symptom, characterised by spasm in arteries or arterioles with cyanosis of skin at tip of nose, lobe of ear, nails etc.

Treatment :

The treatment of RA includes relieving pain and inflammation, joint destruction. Line of treatment is depends upon age, severity of disease and risk factor etc.

1. **Drug treatment :**
   - Non-steroidal anti-inflammatory drugs : Aceclofenac, Diclofenac, Pyroxicam etc.
   - Cox-2 inhibitors : Etoricoxb.
   - Other drugs : Glucosamine, penicillamine etc.
2. **Supportive treatment :** Physiotherapy, Heat therapy and Regular exercise.

4. DIABETES

Diabetes mellitus is a chronic endocrine disorder of carbohydrate, protein, fats metabolism characterised by defective insulin secretion or glucagon. It is caused by increased glucose level (ranges between 80-120 mg%) in the blood, called as hyperglycemia.

A patient with Type - I diabetes mellitus is also known as insulin dependent (IDDM) or having juvenile - onset diabetes.

A patient with Type - II is also known as non-insulin dependent (NIDDM).

Causes of diabetes :

(i) **Hereditary :** It can be transferred to children and grand children.

(ii) **Obesity :** It is one of the most important factors in individual's with family history of diabetes - mellitus.

(iii) **Infections :** Some virus like influenza, mumps and coxsackie destroys β-cells of islet of Langerhans.

Drugs : Some drugs may disturb the release or uptake of insulin e.g. phenytoin, catecholamines, lithium and thyroid preparations.

Pathophysiology :

TYPE – I DM : It results from a genetically suspectible, immune mediated, selective destruction of > 90% of β-cells of islet of Langerhans. Infiltration of T-lymphocytes is accompanied by macrophages and lymphocytes with a lost of β-cells, without involvement of the glucagon secreting α-cells.

TYPE – II DM : It is characterised by hyperglycemia and insulin resistance. Most patients are treated with diet, exercise and oral drugs. The β-cell mass is normal but the pancreatic islet amyloid is due to deposition of amylin in pancreas.

Signs and Symptoms :

(i) Polydipsia - (increase in thirst)

(ii) Loss in body weight with muscular fatigue.

(iii) Polyphagia - (Excessive eating) and polyuria.

(iv) Kitoacidosis, nocturia, blurred vision.
(v) Numbness of feet.
(vi) Slow healing of wounds.
(vii) Retinopathy, lesion of eye.
(viii) Renal failure may occur.

Treatment :

1. The treatment of Diabetes Mellitus initiates by insulin preparations with monodrug therapy.
   - Insulin units by S.C. depending on the gravity DM.
   - Chlorpropamide : 250 mg once.
   - Glibenclamide : 2.5 - 5 mg daily.

2. **Use of oral hypoglycemic agent :** Generally these are prescribed in combination.
   - Glibenclamide + Metformin
     (2.5 – 5 mg) (250 – 500 mg)
   - Glicazide + Metformin
     (80 mg) (500 mg)

3. **Diet control :** Sweets, potato, rice (carbohydrates), excess protein and fat diet consumption is restricted.

5. PEPTIC ULCER

Peptic ulcer disease includes ulceration in the gastrointestinal tract, where the parietal cells secrete hydrochloric acid. Stress ulcer, gastric ulcer, duodenal ulcer and NSAID induced ulcer are most common.

Pathophysiology :

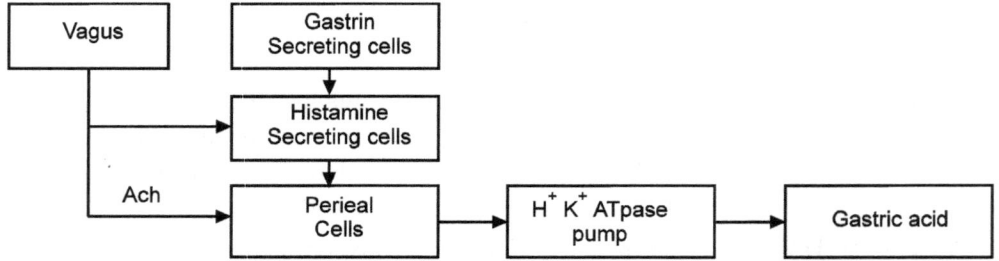

Gastric ulcer occurs at the junction of different epithelial cells and also due to breakdown of the mucosal barrier to back diffusion of acid.

There are different pathways by virtue of their stimulation secrete hyper gastric acid secretion.

(a) Neurocrine pathway : In which acetyl choline stimulates Histamine secreting cells and directly to parietal cells.

(b) **Endocrine pathway** : Activate gastrin secreting cells which act on histamine secreting cell.

(c) **Paracrine pathway** : It stimulates histamine secreting cells via vagus stimulation.

The Histamine acts on the parietal cells. There is a stimulation of hydrogen potassium ATpase pumps which produces gastric acid (hydrochloric acid).

Signs and Symptoms :

(i) Burning sensation of stomach and gastric pain.

(ii) In chronic and recurrent ulcer haemorrage in stomach may occur.

(iii) In some cases there may be anaemia.

(iv) Pain in thorax and upper abdominal region mainly at midnight.

Treatment :

1. Treatment of gastric and peptic ulcer focusses on neutralising or decreasing acidity with :
   - Aluminium hydroxide gel - 5 ml b.i.d.
   - Bismuth subcitrate - 250 mg b.i.d.

2. **Use of H_2 Blockers :**
   - Cemetidine / Rantidine - 400 mg at bed time
   - Famotidine - 40 mg at bed time.

3. **Proton Pump blocker :**
   - Omiprazole = 20 to 40 mg once daily.

4. **Supportive Measures :**
   (a) Avoid alcohol consumption and self medication of NSAID.
   (b) Avoid spicy food.
   (c) Avoid mental stress.

6. CARDIOVASCULAR DISEASES

The cardiovascular system works in a very high tension state. This condition results from the force of contraction of heart muscle to squeeze out the blood and the peripherial resistance produced by the arteries. Apart from this the diet factor, alongwith smoking and liquor, may contribute. Cardiovascular diseases can be categorised as under :

(i) **Congenital** : Atrial Septal Defect (ASD)
Ventricular Septal Defect (VSD)
Stenosis

(ii) **Aquired** : Rheumatic heart fever
Hypertension

(iii) **Ischemic** : Coronary Heart Disease (CHD)
- Angina pectoris
- Myocardial infraction

(iv) **Vascular** :
- Thrombosis
- Embolism
- Arteriosclerosis and Atheoriosclerosis

1. **Congenital Heart Disease :**

Congenital abonormalities of heart occur in the ratio about 8 per 1000 live from birth. It is the most common cause of heart disease in children. This disease covers a broad spectrum of malformations, ranging from small lesion to severe abnormalities that may cause death in adult age. Mainly two factors play a role to cause the disease.

(a) **Genetic factor :** Due to some chromosomal abnormalities, occurrence of familiar forms congenital cardiac malformation are found.

(b) **Environmental factors :** Such as congenital rubella infection is responsible for some cases.

The major forms of congenital heart disease are listed below :
- Atrial Septal Defect (ASD)
- Ventricular Septal Defect (VSD)
- Stenosis : * Pulmonary
             * Aortic
- Tricuspid atresia.

2. **Acquired Heart Diseases :**

Acquired heart dieases are caused by a variety of factors like Diabetes, obesity, lack of exercise, smoking etc.

(a) **Rheumatic heart diseases :** It is caused by rheumatic heart fever, which is caused by a beta haemolytic streptococci. Firstly, it affects the throat, then spreads in joints and finally affects the heart.

(b) **Hypertension :** Hypertension is one of the commonest disorders of cardiovascular system. Blood pressure is an individual is under both genetic and environmental influences. It is measured as systolic and Diastolic B.P., i.e. 120/80 mm Hg is a range. A person whose readings are consistently above 140/90 mm Hg may be said to have hyptertension. The diastolic blood pressure (hypertension) is a classic "silent killer".

Etiology and Pathophysiology :

(i) **Primary hypertension :** It is also called as essential hypertension, more than 90% of the patient with elevation of arterial blood pressure with unknown or no identifiable cause.

In general, increase in blood pressure is regulated by barometric feedback mechanism which includes renin-angiotension and aldosterone, kallikrein-kinin and sympathetic system. Essential hypertension may disturb barostatic messages causing the arterioles to respond improperly.

(ii) **Secondary hypertension :** In this type, the cause of hypertension is known. The causes are as under :

- Acute/Chronic renal diseases.
- Renal artery stenosis.
- Hyperaldosteronism. (endocrine disorder)
- Drug induced hypertension.
    * Oral contraceptives (estrogen, progestins)
    * MAO inhibitors
    * Cyclosporin.

Signs and Symptoms :

(i) Head with tinnitus (ringing sound in the ear)

(ii) Bleeding may occurs from the nose.

(iii) Dizziness and vertigo.

(iv) Odema of optic disk (Papildema) due to increase in intracranial pressure followed by blindness.

(v) Brain haemorrhage.

3. Ischemic Heart Dieases :

It is also called Coronary Heart Disease (CHD), in which there is an imbalance between the myocardial demand and blood supply. The most common cause of ischemic heart disease is a reduction in coronary arterial blood supply due to atheriosclerosis. Various forms of CHD are as under :

- Angina pectoris.
- Mycardial ischemia/infraction.
- Congestive cardiac failure.
- Cardiac failure.

Various factors responsible for CHD are :
- Fat rich diet
- Hypertension
- Diabetes
- Excessive smoking and alcoholic drinks
- Sedentary life with lack of exercise
- Obesity.

Angina Pectoris :

The myocardial ischemia characterised by pericardial discomfort.

Etiology and Pathophysiology :

The cause of Angina, mainly due to obstruction occurs in coronary artery, includes atheriosclerosis, sparm (idiopathic or due to cocaine) and coronary embolism. Apart from this aortic stenosis and calcific aortic stenosis also coats it.

Angina results from the lack of oxygen supply to the mycardium in increased demand condition due to inability of the coronary artery. The myocardium becomes ischemic with localised necrosis. pH of coronary sinus blood falls. Loss of cellular potassium (K^+) may occur. Deterioration of mainly left ventricle may be observed on ECG.

Signs and Symptoms :

(i) Discomfort in the thorax region radiating to trunk, shoulder (left) and lower jaw.

(ii) Myocardial infarction is felt with burning sensation.

(iii) Squeezing and choking sensations.

(iv) Discomfort may be form 30 sec. to 30 min. in case of anginal attack but in myocardial it may persist for few hours.

(v) Nausea, vomitting and headache are very common.

4. Vascular disorder : Atheriosclerosis

Basically, it is a vascular disorder, belonging to a form of artheriosclerosis. Atheriosclerosis characterised by patchy sub-intimal thickening of coronary artery resulting into reduce or obstruct blood flow to the heart.

Pathophysiology : Atherosclerotic plague consists of accumulated intracellular and extracellular lipid, smooth muscle cells, connective tissue. It is initiated with deposition of fatty streak, which later converts into the fibrous plague causes reduced elasticity, that resulting into reduced systolic expansion and abnormally rapid wave propagation.

The development of atherosclerosis comprises :
1. The lipid deposition
2. By chronic endothelial injury.

The lipid deposition hypothesis postulates that, the LDL penetrates into the arterial wall, leading to lipid deposition in smooth muscle cells and in microphages. This deposited LDL then modified or oxidised, which is chemotactic to monocytes, promoting their migration into initima and their early appearance in the form of fatty streak.

Even hypercholesterolemia induces attachment of monocytes to the surface of arterial endothelium produces deposition of lipid, (so called foam cells) and these finally forms fibrous plague.

The chronic endothelical injury occurs by various ways produces loss of :

(a) endothelium

(b) aggregation of platelets

(c) adhesion of platelets

Collectively these forms a fibrous plague.

Signs and Symptoms :

As such atherosclerosis is characteristically silent until other cardiovascular disorder such as thrombosis, aneurysm or embolism supervens.

Symptoms develop gradually as the atheroma. Dramatic signs are observed when major artery is acutely occluded, that causes reduction in blood flow to the affected area of the heart resulting into angina, claudication, myocardial infarction, ischemia etc.

Treatment :

Atherosclerosis's treatment is usually followed at its complications such as :

(a) Agina pectoris   :   • Amlodipine   = 5 mg once daily
                          • Benidipine   = 4 mg b.i.d.
                          • Nifedipine   = 10-40 mg b.i.d.
                          • Diltiazem HCl = 60 mg t.i.d.

(b) Arrhythmia   :   • Iscprenaline
                          • Diltiazem HCl
                          • Adinosine

(c) Myocardial Infarction :
                          • Captopril - Initially 6.25 mg/day
                          • Ramipril - Initially 2.5 mg b.i.d.
                          • Cardiotonic (Digoxin)

(d) **Atherosclerotic form :**

Lopid lowering agent   +   Antihypertensive
- Atorvastatin = 10 – 20 mg daily
- Fenofibrate = 160 mg daily
- Alogrithm
- Atenolol = 50 – 100 mg once daily
- Perindopril = 4 mg once daily
- Amlodipine = 5 mg once daily

7. EPILEPSY

Epilepsy is a chronic, functional disorder of the nervous system. It is usually associated with loss of consciousness by recurrent, generalised transient, seizures having onset and spontaneous resolution.

Epidemiology : The occurrence of disorder is highest in the first 10 years of life and minimise thereafter till the age of 50. The reasons for death with epilepsy includes accident, tumors, cerebro-vascular disorders, suicide etc.

Pathophysiology : Seizures may occur due to primary or acquired abnormalities of CNS functions, metabolic disturbances and number of systemic disorders.

Seizures result due to an imbalance of excitatory and inhibitory influences within the brain. GABA (γ-amino butaric acid), sodium channel and potassium channel plays a role in depolarization, which follows by hyperpolarization which results into eflux of extracellular ion (calcium) this burts of action potentials are the originating effect of a seizure.

The seizures are of two types :

(a) **Generalised seizures :** This involves the entire cerebral cortex resulting into following forms :

  (i) *Grand mal epilepsy* : In this type, there is sudden loss of consciousness, falling of individual, tonic then clonic jerks of muscles. The unconscious state lasts for about 30 min. After awakening the patient cannot recollect the events of the proceedings.

  (ii) *Petit mal epilepsy* : In this, the unconscious state remains for few seconds only. Jerk of arms with blinking eye-lid may be observed. The patient cannot show facial movement.

(b) **Partial seizures :** This involves the focal brain lesions. There are two categories among the partial seizures.

  (i) **Simple partial seizures :** In this, there is no loss of consciousness and the manifestations depend on the site of brain lesion. If it be motor part involves contraction of body part or sensory part causes numbness to one part of the body.

(ii) **Complex partial seizures** : Also called as psychomotor seizures. The lesion occurs in temporal region of brain, causes sudden environment/ emotional changes like smell, feelings followed by the loss with surrounding. It lasts for few minutes.

Treatment :

Long-term therapy is for atleast 3 years sometimes life time.

1. Treatment initiated with :
   - Carbamazepine - 100 to 200 mg b.i.d.
   - Clonazepam - initially 1 mg at night.
   - Fosphenytoin - 15 mg/kg by I.V.
   - Sodium velproate.
2. Occasionally used drugs :
   - Phenobarbital
   - Clobazam.

QUESTIONS

1. Describe pathophysiology, signs and symptoms of Tuberculosis.
   [(S - 04, 02, 97, 96 : W - 03, 00, 99) 4 marks]
2. What are the disease manifestations due to hepatitis ?
   [(S - 03, 01, 00 : W - 99) 4 marks]
3. State the signs and symptoms of Rhumatoid arthritis.
   [(W - 00, 97) 4 marks]
4. What are the manifestations of Diabetes ?
   [(S - 03, 02, 01 : W - 03) 4 marks]
5. Write pathophysiology of peptic ulcer. **[(S - 02, 99 : W - 02, 00) 4 marks]**
6. Explain Angina pectoris alongwith signs and symptoms. **[(W - 01) 4 marks]**
7. Classify cardio vascular disease with manifestations. **[(W - 03) 4 marks]**
8. Explain pathophysiology and types of epilepsy.

■■■

5

PHYSIOLOGICAL PARAMETERS

(The Gauges)

INTRODUCTION

Perhaps life is the most mysterious and dynamic existence in the universe. The human body comprises different types of cells, tissues and systems. These have a specific important physiological parameter, in performing bio-chemical and bio-physical reaction to maintain normal physiology of the body. But any type of deviation in these parameters shows abnormality in that part or system function. So a clinical pharmacist may be essential to study physiological parameters because of the link between the physician and the patient.

Definition :

Physiological parameters can be defined as the gauges used to check normal physiological form of organ/orangelle system.

(A) Haematological Parameters :

1. **RBC (Red Blood Cell) Count :** Total RBC count reports the number of RBCs found in a cu/mm of whole blood. The normal values of RBC's in human blood is :

   Male   : 5 millions/cumm
   Female   : 4.0 – 4.5 millions/cumm
   Infants   : 6.0 – 7.0 millions/cumm
   Foetus   : 8.0 millions/cumm

   Significance: Increase in number of RBC count indicates polycythaemia due to dehydration, exercise, lack of oxygen etc.

   Decrease in RBC count shows anaemia, leukemia, old age, (haemolytic poison) snake poisoning.

   (a) **Packed Cell Volume (PVC) or Haematocrit (Hct) :** It gives % by volume of packed RBCs in the whole sample after centrifugation. The normal value is :

   Male   : 0.4 – 0.54
   Female   : 0.37 – 0.47

   Significance: Increase in PCV indicates polycythemia or dehydration.

   Decrease in PCV indicates anaemia or over hydration.

(b) Mean Corpuscular Volume (MCV) : It is the ratio of the Hct to RBC count.

$$MCV = \frac{Hct\% \times 10}{RBC\ count}$$

The size of RBC is determined by MCV. The normal value is 75-99 fl in adult male and female.

Significance : An increase in MCV indicates macrocytic anaemia due to Vit. B-12 and folic acid deficiencies.

A decrease in MCV reflects microcytic anaemia due to iron deficiency.

(c) Haemoglobin (Hb) : The test counts the amount of haemoglobin (gm/dL) of whole blood and gives idea of oxygen carrying capacity of blood. A decrease amount of Hb causes anaemia. The normal value is

Male   : 14 – 16 gm%

Female   : 12 – 15 gm%

Infants   : 16 – 18 gm%

Significance : An increase % Hb indicates polycythaemia and dehydration.

An decrease % Hb reflects anaemia and leukemia.

(d) Colour Index : It is defined as relative amount of haemoglobin present in a single RBC.

$$Colour\ Index = \frac{Hb\%}{RBC\%}$$

Normal colour index is 0.85 to 1.5.

Significance : If colour index is less than 0.85, it describes hypochromic anaemia.

If colour index is more than 1.15, it indicates hyperchromic anaemia.

(e) ESR (Erythrocyte Sedimentation Rate) : Erythrocytes have a tendency to settle down because of their greater density than plasma and roulex formation.

If a blood with anticoagulant is placed in a long vertical tube the sedimentation of erythrocytes occurs leaving a small clear plasma at the top. It is measured as mm/hour. It is generally measured by two methods with normal value.

Method	ESR mm/hr.	
	Male	Female
Wintrobe	3 – 5	4 – 7
Westergren	0 – 9	0 – 12

Significance : Despite the diagnostic tool, ESR is preferred for its *prognostic* value for diseases. ESR shows increased in conditions like tuberculosis, leukaemia, pneumonia, rheumatoid, arthritis, malignant tumour and myocardial infarction.

ESR shows decrease in polycythaemia, sickle cell anaemia etc.

Advantages :

(i) ESR is useful to follow the clinical course of a disease.

(ii) To distinguish diseases which have almost the same signs and symptoms.

e.g. *Angina pectoris* shows no change in ESR *Myocardial infarction* indicates increase in ESR.

2. **WBC (White Blood Cells; Leukocytes) :** The WBC or total Leukocyte (TLC) count states the number of WBC in a per cumm of whole blood. The normal value of WBC are as follows :

    Adult   :   4000 – 10000 per cumm

    Children : 6000 – 11000 per cumm

    Infants   : 8000 – 13000 per cumm

    New born : 10000 – 20000 per cumm

Significance : An **increase** in the WBC count causes Leukocytosis due to infection.

A **decrease** in count of WBC leads to Leukopenia due to viral infection or toxic effects of drugs.

DLC Count : The differential Leukocytes (WBC) count gives the distribution and Morphology. Granulocytes (Neutrophils, Eosinphils and Basophiles) and Agranulocytes (Monocytes and Lymphocytes).

The normal ranges of differential leukocytes is as below :

Name of Leukocyte	% count	Absolute count cumm
Neutrophils	60 – 70%	2500 – 7000
Eosinophils	1 – 4%	40 – 400
Basophils	0 – 1%	0 – 100
Monocytes	4 – 8%	150 – 800
Lymphocytes	20 – 30%	1000 – 3000

Significance :

Neutrophillia (increase in neutrophils count)

(i) This response may occur in viral infections (e.g. chicken pox herpes zoster, small pox).

(ii) In acute bacterial infections like urinary tract infections, pneumonia, whooping cough, septicemia.

(iii) In inflammatory diseases like rheumatoid arthritis, gout, acute rheumatic fever.

Neutropenia (Decrease in neutrophilis count)

(i) In infections like typhoid, influenza, kala azar miliary tuberculosis.

(ii) In gangrenous ulcer of mouth and throat.

Basophillia (Increase in basophils count)

(i) In acute viral infections like mumps, chicken pox, hepatitis.

(ii) Chronic infections increases of tuberculosis, syphilis, pertassis.

(iii) In haemopoietic disorders like Lymphocytic leukemia.

(iv) Carcinoma of breast also shows increase in count of basophils.

Eosinophilia (An increase in esosinophils count)

(i) Allergic disorders like asthma, hay fever, eczema, food allergy shows increase in count.

(ii) Chronic skin diseases, jaundice and leprosy may increase count of eosinophils .

(iii) Parasitic infection caused by ring worms, hook worms also increases the count.

(iv) Haemopoietic disorder such as anaemias, Hodgkins disease and leukaemia.

Eosinopenia (A decrease in number of count) :

(i) In some acute infections, stress situation.

(ii) In cushing disease (hyperfunctioning of adrenal cortex)

Monocytosis (Increase in count of monocytes) :

It may occur in tuberculosis, subacute endocarditis, monocytic leukaemia, typhoid fever, kala-azar Hodgkins disease etc.

Lymphocytosis (An increased number of lymphocytes)

(i) Acute viral infections mumps, chicken pox and viral hepatitis shows increase in number of lymphocytes.

(ii) Chronic infections such as tuberculosis, pertusis, syphilis and lymphocytic leukaemia.

Lymphopenia (Count of Lymphocyte is decreased)

In AIDS, immunodeficiency states, renal failures, Hodgkins disease etc.

3. **Thrombocytes (Platelets) :**

Thrombocytes are the fractional formed element of blood and are involved in blood clotting after vascular injury. The normal range for thrombocyte count is :

$$1,50,000 - 3,00,000 \text{ per cumm.}$$

Thrombocytopenia results from decreased production of platelets, may result from bone marrow disfunctioning.

Thrombocytosis occurs from increased production of platelets, may result from inflammatory disorders, blood disorders and malignancy etc.

(a) **Bleeding Time :** Bleeding time is a measurement of haemostatic efficiency of blood. It is determined as the time required to cease the haemorrhages from a puncture wound. The normal value of bleeding time ranges from
1 to 3 min.

Significance : (i) It is related with platelet functional disorders.

(ii) Long course of anticoagulants or Aspirin.

(b) **Clotting time :** Clotting time is a vitro testing of the haemostatic efficiency of blood. It is the time required to clot the blood outside the body. The normal value of clotting time ranges from **4 to 10 min.**

Significance : Increase in clotting time indicates haemophilia (Deficiency of factor XIII) OR presence of circulating anticoagulants.

(B) Biochemical Parameters :

1. **Blood sugar :** The blood contains a certain amount of sugar to provide energy to the body to perform various functions. The normal fasting blood sugar level is ranging from **80 – 120 mg%**. If blood sugar level falls below 70 or 50 mg % the symptoms of hypoglycemia appear. An increase level is known as hyperglycemia.

    Significance : The increased level of blood sugar is indicative of diabetes, severe nephritis, hepatic and pancreatic disorders, hyperthyroidism etc.

    Low level of sugar reflects insulin administration, chronic alcoholism. In conditions like hypothyroidism, creatinism etc.

2. **Blood Cholesterol :** Blood cholesterol level measurement comprises an important test for those patient suffering from cardiovascular diseases. The normal value of blood cholesterol is **120 – 240 mg %**. It is directly related with ageing and reaches 280 – 300 mg among 70 years old people.

    Significance : Cholesterol is present in the following forms :

    (i) **LDL cholesterol :** Means low density lipoprotein cholesterol 60 - 80% of total cholesterol.

    (ii) **HDL cholesterol :** Means High Density lipoprotein cholesterol 25 - 40% of total cholesterol.

Cholesterol level mg %	Diseases
80 – 100	Pernicious anaemia, hyperthyroidism
300 – 400	Coronary disease like atheriosclerosis
400 – 500	Diabetes
500 – 600	Obstructive jaundice
Above 600	Nephrosis

3. **Lipid profile :** The patients, who are at the high risk of cardiovascular disorders, essentially to know the status of level of lipid profile, which consists the measurement of cholesterol, triglycerides, low and high density lipoproteins and risk ratio such as cholesterol : HDL and LDL : HDL.

Estimation	Normal value
Serum total cholesterol	120 - 240 mg%
Serum triglycerides	60 - 165 mg%
Serum HDL	30 - 90 mg%
Serum LDL	80 - 150 mg%
Serum VLDL	upto 35 mg%
Risk ratio :	
Cholesterol : HDL	3 to 6
LDL : HDL	upto 3.5

In general, increased lipid profile shows hyperlipo-proteinemia.

Significances :

- In alcoholic cirrhosis the lipid profile is remain on higher side.
- The LDL value is found to be higher in case of atheriosclerosis, impaired glucose tolerance and acute relapsing pancreatitis.
- Triglyceride level increases in hyperthyroidism and CHD.
- LDL : HDL ratio increases in diabetes.

4. **Serum enzymes :** It is also an important gauze to diagnose few diseases. Despite the presence of enzymes in fractional amounts, they may release in large amount on tissue damage. Some of the enzymes are discussed in the following table :

Sr. No.	Enzyme	Normal value	Significance
1.	Creatine Phosphokinase (CPK) OR Creatine Kinase (CK)	Men : 20 - 50 IU Women : 10 - 37 IU	Increased level found in myocardial infarction, polymotis, motor nurone disorders, muscular dystrophy.
2.	Lactic acid dehydrogenase (LDH or LD)	70 - 240 IU	Level increased in obstructive jaundice, viral hepatitis, acute pancreatitis and in anaemias.

Contd. ...

3.	Alkaline Phosphatase (ALP)	Adult : 29 - 92 IU Children : 90 - 220 IU	Level increases in liver diseases, rickets and osteomalacia.
4.	Serum Glutamic Oxaloacetic Transaminase (SGOT) OR Aspirate transaminase (AST)	Men : 0 - 40 IU Women : 0 - 30 IU	Ischemic heart diseases, jaundice, viral hepatitis etc. shows increased level.
5.	Serum Glutamic Pyruvic Transaminase (SGPT) OR Alanine Transminase (ALT)	5 - 35 IU	Level increases in severe hepatitis and hepatic damages. In dermatomyositis.

(C) Patho-Clinical Parameters :

1. **Urine analysis :** Urine is examined physically, chemically and microscopically to obtain information regarding renal function or some systemic diseases.

(a) Physical Tests		Specification	Significance
(i)	Volume	350 – 500 ml	All these reflects the urine sample is physiological, otherwise it is pathological.
(ii)	Appearance	Clear, faint yellow	
(iii)	Odour	Aromatic	
(iv)	Specific gravity	1.03 – 1.02	
(v)	pH (Reaction)	Slightly acidic	
(b) Chemical tests		Normal value	Significance
(i)	Sugar (Glucose)	Abnormal constituents	Glycosuria (Diabetes)
(ii)	Protein (Albumin)	Abnormal constituents	Proteinuria (Albuminuria) High protein meal Pyelonephritis Nephritis and Pregnancy

Contd. ...

(iii)	**Bile salts :** Taurocholate - Na Glycocholate - Na	Abnormal constituents	Jaundice
(iv)	**Bile pigments :** Billirubin Billiverdin	Abnormal constituents	Jaundice
(v)	**Ketone bodies**	Abnormal constituents	Ketonuria (ketosis). In starvation diabetes (Hypoglycemia)
(vi)	**Blood cells**	Abnormal constituents	Haematuria. Haemolysis due to poison kidney diseases, cancer etc.
(c) Microscopic Tests		**Normal value**	**Significance**
(i)	Epithelial cells	Traces in normal urine	Haemorrhagic and degenerative nephritis
(ii)	Pus cells	Traces in normal urine	RBC with pus reflects pyelonephritis.
(iii)	Crystals	Appears after long time	Chances of renal calculi
(iv)	Casts	Trace in normal urine	Renal Irritation causes increased amount.

2. **Stool Examination :** It is also examined in similar fashion of testing as physical, chemical and microscopic to evaluate GIT disorder and infectious diseases.

(a) Physical Tests		**Normal value**	**Significance**
(i)	Nature	Semisolid	Liquid form in pathogenic bacterial and amoeba infection.
(ii)	Colour	Brownish	Internal haemorrhage may change the colour.
(iii)	Odour	Characteristic	Foul odour due to ulcer to rectum.
(iv)	Mucous	Very less amount	Excess loss of mucous in amoebic dysentry and colitis.

Contd....

(b) Chemical test	Normal value	Significance
Similar to urine analysis	–	–
(c) Microscopic Tests	**Normal value**	**Significance**
1. Cells	–	Amoebic dysentry : mucous, pus cells, RBC's. Bacillary dysentry : pus cells and macrophages.
2. Parasites and eggs	–	Various protozoa's like E-Coli and worms.

3. **Cerebro-Spinal Fluid (CSF) Analysis :** C.S.F. is formed by the selective dialysis of plasma by choroid plexus of ventricles of the brain, and it travels into the sub-arachonoid space of the brain and spinal cord. The CSF has a defined nature and composition, which is summarized as :

Physical Properties	Chemical composition
Appearance : Clear	Proteins : 15 - 45 mg/dl
Colour : Colourless	Albumin : 50 - 70%
pH : 7.3 to 7.4	Globulin : 30 - 50%
Specific gravity : 1.003 to 1.008	Glucose : 40 - 80 mg/dl
	Cholesterol : 0.2 to 0.6 mg/dl
	Creatinine : 0.5 - 1.2 mg/dl
	Urea : 6 - 16 g/dl
	Uric acid : 0.5 - 4.5 mg/dl
	Inorganics Cl^- : 700 - 750 mg/dl
	K^+ : 2 - 3.5 mEg/L
	Na : 144 - 154 mEg/L

The C.S.F. examine mainly for the diagnosis of bacterial, viral or haemorrhagic disorders.

Test	Normal value	Significance
Appearance	Cloudy to purulent clot Cloudy fibrin web Xanthocrome	Observed in acute meningitis. It is seen tuberculous meningitis. It indicates cerebral haemorrhage.

Glucose	Low value (0 - 40 mg/dl)	In case of bacterial or fungal infection or acute meningitis.
	High value	In brain tumor the value rises.
Proteins	High value	In tuberculous meningitis and cerebral haemorrhage.
Chlorides	Low value	It is found in tuberculous meningitis.

(D) Supportive Parameters :

1. **Heart rate OR Pulse rate :** It measures the pulse per unit of time and can be defined as the wave of expansion and elongation produced in the wall of aorta and passed on all the arteries of the body. Generally, the radical artery at the wrist region is used to measure the heart rate.

   The normal heart rate at different stages of life is as under :

   The normal heart rate in adult is 70-80/min.

   Foetus   : 140 – 150 / min
   Childs   : 100 – 120 / min
   Adults   : 70 – 80 / min
   Old   : 60 – 75 / min.

   Significance : Heart rate helps to observe the myocardial status and status of blood pressure. It increases in fear, shock, excitement, exercise, fever etc. and the condition is referred as tachycardia. And bradycardia is decreased heart rate.

2. **Respiration rate :** The normal rate of respiration in adult is 14 - 18 per min. It is higher in children and still higher in infants.

   Significance : It increases in metabolic rate, Pyrexia, exercise, cardiovascular **disorders**, excitement etc.

3. **Blood pressure :** It is defined as the lateral pressure of blood exerted on the walls of blood vessel. The arterial blood pressure has different phases.

   - **Systolic pressure :** It is the maximum pressure during the systole of heart (called as SP).
   - **Diastolic pressure :** It is the maximum pressure during the diastole of heart (called as DP).

- **Pulse pressure :** It is the difference between the systolic and diastolic blood pressure (called as PP)

Normal Range of BP	Std. BP
SP : 110 – 140 mm Hg	SP : 120 mm Hg
DP : 70 – 90 mm Hg	DP : 80 mm Hg
PP : 40 – 55 mm Hg	PP : 40 mm Hg

Significance : Increase B.P. leads to a condition known as "hypertension" due to stress, atheriosclerosis, arteriosclerosis, diabetes and ageing process. It rises above 150 / 95 mm Hg.

Decreased condition is hypotension due to anaemias, haemorrhages or peripheral vasodilation, organo-phosphorus poisoning and shock etc. It measures as below normal value.

4. **Body temperature :** Human being is homoitherm (warm blooded animal) and hence the ability to regulate own body temperature. The normal value is between 97°F – 99°F The rise in body temperature leads to a condition called pyrexia or fever.

Significance : It is a valuable symptom of illness, occurs due to dearrangement of heat regulating mechanism. Toxins, infections, dehydration, blood pressure etc. raises body temperature.

(E) Functional Parameters :

Organs like liver and kidney plays a vital role in maintaining homeostatis of the body. Abnormality in functioning of such organ results from microbial infections, disorders or diseases. Mainly it includes two functional tests are as :

1. Liver Function Test (LFT) : Liver is the bio-engine, associated with maintaining of homeostatis. Thus, the disfunction of liver is co-related with disorders or diseases of other organs/systems too. Hence, some essential tests are performed, discussed below :

Sr. No.	Test	Normal value	Significance
1.	Alkaline Phosphatase (ALP)	Refer B - 4, 3	
2.	Serum bilirubin	0.3 - 1.3 mg%	Level increases in jaundice

3.	Serum proteins		
	Total	5 - 8 mg%	Total protein count decreases in acute infectious disease hyperthyroidism and diabetes mellitus.
	Albumin	3 - 6 mg%	
	Globulin	1.5 - 3 mg%	
4.	SGOT and SGPT	Refer B - 3, 4 & 5	
5.	Serum cholesterol	Refer B - 2	
6.	Prothrombin time	12 to 16 seconds	It increases due to the lack of vitamin e K, which is synthesized by liver. Thus, shows hepatocellular diseases.

2. Kidney Function Test (KFT) : The various functions of kidney are dearranged in pre-renal and post-renal conditions. So, it is checked by performing some test. It is also referred as Renal Function Test (RFT).

Sr. No.	Test	Normal value	Significance
1.	Creatine clearance test	1 - 2 mg%	Value decreases in renal failure.
2.	Urea clearance test	10 - 12 mg%	Glomerular structure status is indicated.
3.	Uric acid	Male : 3.4 to 7 mg% Female : 2.4 to 7 mg%	Increase value shows signs of Rheumatoid arthritis/gout
4.	Serum Na^+ Ka^+	135 – 155 mmol./lit. 3.5 to 5.5 mmol/lit.	Increase level shows the diminishing of reabsorption at renal tubules.

(F) Gonadal Parameters :

Sperm count : The semen examination is one of the important clinical parameter of gonadal function. A normal semen is practically valuable for normal androgenicity. Spermatozoa (sperm) are the only cells type present in it, the sperms are stored in vas-deferens and released during ejaculation. Therefore, the normal sperm count is essential for fertility.

Normal count : 100 - 150 millions/c.c. of semen.

Significance of count : Person with low count might show infertility.

QUESTIONS

1. What is the significance of ESR ? [S - 03, 97]
2. Write a note on importance of DLC. [S - 04, 01]
3. What are physiological parameters ? Do they help in diagnosis of diseases ? Explain with two suitable examples. [S - 00 : W - 00, 97]
4. Give normal value of : [W - 00, 99, 96 : S - 03, 02, 97, 96]
   - (i) Blood sugar level of **
   - (ii) ESR**
   - (iii) Cholesterol**
   - (iv) Pulse rate**
   - (v) Respiration**
   - (vi) WBC count
   - (vii) Cosinophils
   - (viii) Basophils
   - (ix) RBC**
   - (x) Specific gravity of urine
   - (xi) Clotting time
   - (xii) Hb.

** No. of times asked.

6

DRUG INTERACTIONS

(The Vitro)

INTRODUCTION

Day by day development of new therapeutic, chemotherapeutic or other category drugs are raising challenges to clinical field. However, accompanying the pharmacological actions, produced by the use of these drugs also created its related problems in the form of unpredictable adverse reactions.

The phenomenon of drug interaction cannot be correlated with drug or therapeutic incompatibility, because it occurs merely due to pharmacokinetic or pharmacodynamic changes taking place inside the body.

Drug interactions can be defined as "the effects of drugs altered by another drug or food that is prior or concurrent administration with it". Then it is termed as Drug-Drug or Drug-food interaction.

Classification :

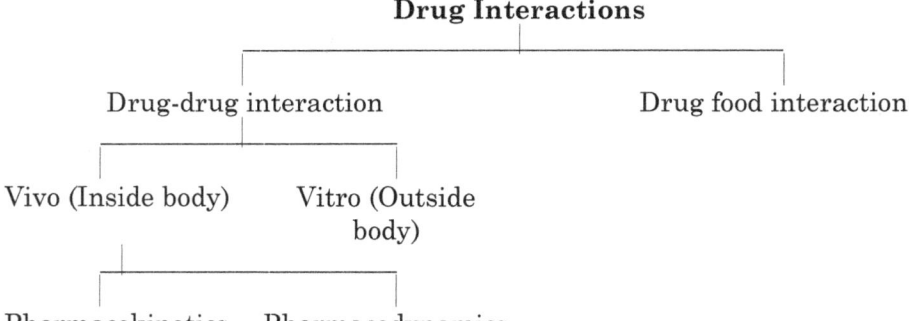

Reasons of Drug interaction :

1. **Use of OTC drugs :** Without consultation of a physician use of OTC drugs like aspirin, antacids nasal decongestant etc. with prescribed drugs can result into drug-drug interaction.

2. **Patient's non-compliance :** Many patients do not adhere to the instructions of prescriber or pharmacists advices on prescribed drugs. e.g. A diabetic patient is strictly adviced to prevent alcoholic drinks/liquor to avoid further hypoglycemic crises.

3. **Multiple physicians :** A patient receiving a treatment from multiple physicians for different illnesses. e.g. patient taking anticholinergic for GIT disorder Neostigmine and physostigmine for ophthalmic purpose.

4. **Drug Abuse or misuse :** A thinking of patient that more consumption of drug will produce quick relief, can result into drug interactions.

5. **Potent Drugs :** May produce many pharmacological actions on different physiological systems or system's organs is one of the causes to produce drug interaction.

Role of Pharmacist in drug interactions

A pharmacist is well-versed with pharmacokinetics and pharmacodynamics of drugs. He is ideal person who can play a vital role in preventing interactions of drug by advising the patient on the following :

1. Do not use OTC drugs without the consultation of a physician.
2. Strictly follow the instructions given by the physician regarding administration timings and doses.
3. If receiving treatment from multiple physicians inform them, about the illnesses before taking the medicines.
4. Do not consume drugs in excess apart from recommended dose.
5. Do not take different drugs at once.
6. Which type of food is forbidden for a particular drug.

Mechanism of Drug interaction :

The mechanism of drug interaction comprises pharmacokinetic and pharmacodynamics which means what the body does to the drug and drug does to the body respectively. Kinetic includes drug absorption, distribution, metabolism and elimination, whereas pharmacodynamics are the numerous actions of drug on the body systems or their organs. The mechanisms are discussed below:

1. Pharmacokinetics :

(a) G.I.T. Absorption : Delay in absorption or interference with it, affects the onset of action of the drug. Number of factors alter the process of absorption as given below :

(i) **Change in pH :** Acidic drugs are readily absorbed from stomach, because they remain in unionised form e.g. salicylates. Basic drugs are easily absorbed from the intestine.

(ii) **Adsorption or complexation of drug :** Activated charcoal and kaolin act as adsorbents so are given in case of poisoning and diarrhoea to adsorb unabsorbed poison and bacterial toxins etc.

(iii) **GIT Status :** Decrease in GIT motility and emptying rate alters the rate of adsorption. e.g. Decrease in motility increase absorption of drugs like prednisone and digoxin. Increase in emptying rate decreases the absorption of drugs.

(iv) **Other factors :** Presence of other agents either favours or decreases the absorption of drug.

(b) **Alternation in Distribution :** Affinity and efficacy of a drug to bind with plasma proteins alters the displacement from protein binding site. Some examples are given in the following table :

Drug bind with protein	Displacing Drug	Effect
1. Tolbutamide	Salicylates	Hypoglycemia
2. Warfarin	Phenyl-butazone	Haemorrhages
3. Methotrexate	Salicylates and sulpha	Agranulocytosis

(c) **Change in metabolism :** "Enzyme induction" i.e. increase in enzymatic activity enhances fate of drug, which decreases the therapeutic effect of the drug.

Alcohol, phenytoin, chloral hydrate are enzyme - inducing drugs.

"Enzyme inhibition" i.e. decrease in enzymatic activity prolongs the fate of drug, thereby increasing the effect of drug.

There are drugs that inhibit enzyme activity like chloramphenicol, cimetidine, metronidazole, isoniazide.

(d) **Change in excretion :**

(i) **pH of urine :** Ionised drugs easily diffuse and are excreted in the urine. So, any drug that changes pH of urine affects excretion of weak acid or weak bases.

(ii) **Competitive excretion :** Renal tubular transport between concurrently administered drugs generally changes excretion of one other.

2. **Pharmacodynamic Interaction :**

(a) **Drugs having opposing pharmacological actions (Antagonism) :** Taking at a time, two drugs, having opposite pharmacological actions is called antagonisms and may be given to the patient by physicians for different illnesses. e.g. oxyphenonium (anticholinergic) prescribed for antispasmodic action and at the same time a patient is receiving a treatment from ophthalmologist with prescribed drugs like pilocarpine.

(b) Drugs having similar pharmacological actions (Synergism) : When two drugs are given at a time to the patient which act on same physiological system this results into additive or synergestic effect.

e.g. procain and paracetamol on injectable administration found synergestic in Chikun gunea.

(i) A combination of ephedrine and aminophyllin for asthma.

(ii) Procaine and adrenaline increase in duration of action of procaine.

(iii) Ca ions give synergisms with digitoxin in hypodynamic heart.

(c) Drug competition at receptor site : This may occur at the same receptor's site with same targeted organ. The effect is produced after binding of a drug at receptor site. Two drugs administered together may compete to bind with same receptor and it depends on :

(i) The availability of free site at receptor binding.

(ii) The affinity of both the drugs for the receptor binding.

e.g. Timatol maleate used in glaucoma whereas Lebetalol is used as antihypertensive both produce their actions after binding with β-2 receptor site.

(d) Change of electrolyte level : The effect of a drug can be modified due to change in fluid and electrolyte level.

e.g. Diuretics increases excretion of potassium, may cause hypokalemia; the patient on cardiotonics like digitalis needs monitoring because the heart becomes more sensitive to digitalis.

DRUG - DRUG INTERACTION

(A) Analgesic Drug Interactions :

Sr. No.	Combination	Mechanism of Interaction	Clinical significance
1.	Aspirin and probenecid	Both compete for same binding site on plasma albumin.	Uricosuric action of probenecid is decreased. Aspirin can not be given in gout with probensecid.

2.	Aspirin and Heparin, Warfarin (Anticoagulants)	Aspirin potentiates the activity of anticoagulants by interfering with binding site and decreasing platelets (thrombocytes) activity.	Chances of mucosal bleeding are very high. e.g. Nesal and gastric. During oral anticoagulant therapy, aspirin should be avoided.
3.	Aspirin and urine alkalinizer	Change in pH of urine towards alkaline, which inhibits re-absorption of aspirin at renal tubules.	Aspirin's serum concentration (level) is reduced. A physician should not prescribe both these drugs at a time.

(B) Diuretic Drug Interactions :

Sr. No.	Combination	Mechanism of Interaction	Clinical significance
1.	Frusemide, Thiazides and Antidiabetics	The action of sulphonyl ureas antagonizes, the loss of potassium may also be responsible for this effect.	Patient should be given potassium supplement. A diabetic patient should be monitored and substituting less diabetogenic diuretic.
2.	Thiazides and Antihypertensive	Diuretics potentiate effect of methyl-dopa and guanethedine.	This combination is valuable for the physician. The patient should be monitored for excessive hypotension.
3.	Thiazides, Acetazolamide and Quinidine	Diuretics makes urine alkaline, results into increase in reabsorption of quinidine at renal tubules.	Thiazides shows additive effect with quinidine's parenteral administration. Care should be taken for urine alkalinisation during quinidine therapy.

(C) Cardiovascular drugs interaction :

Sr. No.	Combination	Mechanism of Interaction	Clinical significance
1.	**Cardiac glycoside** Digitalis and Antacids	GIT absorption of cardiotonics is impaired by Aluminium hydroxyl gel or magnesium trisilicate.	Therapeutic level of digoxin may not be achieved. The interval between both the drugs administration timing should be long enough.
2.	**Antihypertensive** Propranolol and Antidiabetics	Inhibits conversion of glycogen to glucose from liver resulting into hypoglycemia	Hypertension and bradycardia during hypoglycemia. Physician should reduce dose of antidiabetic agent.
3.	**Antiarrhythmics** Guanethidine and Amitriptyline, nortriptyline	Antipsychotics antagonises the action of antiarrythmics.	Avoid tricyclic anti-depressants.

(D) Gastrointestinal agents interaction :

Sr. No.	Combination	Mechanism of Interaction	Clinical significance
1.	Antacid and Aspirin	Antacid reduces GIT irritation by neutralising hyperacid secretion induced by aspirin.	Facilitates absorption of aspirin. This combination can be useful to the physician in case of patient with acidity syndrome.
2.	Antacid and Antritubercular agent	Aluminium hydroxide gel adsorbs Isoniazide	Decrease in bio-availability of isoniazide. Antacid may be given after some interval.
3.	Purgatives and poorly absorbed drugs	Cathartics increase motility of intestine which increase rate of passing of drug through GIT.	Decreased absorption of drug. Concurrent administration with purgative of other drug shall be avoided.

(E) Vitamins interactions :

Sr. No.	Combination	Mechanism of Interaction	Clinical significance
1.	Cynocobalamine (Vit. B_{12}) and chloramphenicol	Chloramphenicol interfaces with erythrocyte maturity.	Patient with pernicious anaemia respond poorly to Vit. B_{12} if chloramphenicol is given with.
2.	Vit. A (Retinol) and Mineral oil	Mineral oils decrease absorption of Vit. A from G.I.T.	Separate doses of oil and Vit. are given.

(F) Antidiabetic agent interaction :

Sr. No.	Combination	Mechanism of Interaction	Clinical significance
1.	Antidiabetic agent and alcohol	Alcohol has hypoglycemic effect, thus severe hypoglycemia may occur	Alcohol should be completely avoided.
2.	Antidiabetic agent and oral contraceptives	Impaired glucose tolerance may occur	Oral contraceptives replaced by other than oral.
3.	Tolbutamide + Insuline + Aspirin	Aspirin displaces protein binding of Tolbutomide and then sudden effect of tolbutamide results.	Sudden decrease of glucose level.

Vitro (Drug-Drug interaction outside the body)

These types of interactions occurs when two or more drugs are mixed during intravenous infusion. One drug may be inactivated before it enters the body.

e.g. Concurrent administration of heparin and tetracycline in infusion results in inactivation of tetracycline.

Drug-Food Interactions

In case of oral administration of drug, food may alter the absorption of drug by comprising :

(a) Dilution of drug

(b) Adsorption or complexation of drug.

(c) Change in gastric emptying.

e.g.

1. Milk reduces absorption of tetracycline by forming an insoluble complex.

2. Fatty food delays gastric emptying time and alters rate of absorption.

3. MAO inhibitors, if are administered with tyramine (amine) containing food like cheese and butter severe hypertension can result in death.

4. Absorption of some drugs reduces in presence of food e.g. Ampicillin, Rifampicin, Isoniazide.

5. Absorption of drugs like riboflavin, spironolactone, carbamazepine increases in presence of food.

QUESTIONS

1. What are drug interactions ? Explain the role of pharmacist in identifying and preventing drug interactions. **[(W - 20) 4 marks]**

2. Describe pharmacokinetic interaction with examples.
[(S - 04, 02, 96, 97 : W - 01) 4 marks]

3. What is meant by pharmacodynamics drug interaction ? Give examples.
[(S - 03, 97, 96] 4 marks]

4. What is food drug interaction ? Explain with example.
[(S - 02, 01, 99, 96) 4 marks]

■■■

7

ADVERSE DRUG REACTIONS

(The Consequences)

INTRODUCTION

Medicine can be used to prevent or treat the disease or illness. However, few times it can cause trouble. Such troubles are called adverse drug reactions. The drug has the ability to produce many effects, but the physician mainly wants a patient to experience only one of them; and remaining effects may be considered as undesired. The term "ADR" is more appropriate for effects that are undesired, unpleasant, noxious or potentially harmful.

There are many definitions to describe an adverse drug reactions; but WHO (World Health Organisation) defined it as a response to a drug which is noxious or unwanted and occurs at dosages normally used in human being for prophylaxis, diagnosis or therapy of disease OR for the modification of any physiological function.

Adverse drug reactions are more frequent in patients those who take self medication in large number of drugs with doses or treatment taking at once from physicians for different ailments.

For example : Expectorent which contains Antihistaminic drug produces drowziness in large doses; and it is self-medicated in a age group of 22 to 30 years old.

Classification of Adverse Drug Reaction : They are summarised as below :

Adverse drug reactions

1. Predictable	2. Unpredictable
1.1 Other effects (Quantitative intolerence)	2.1 Qualitative intolerance
1.1.1 Excessive Pharmacological actions	2.1.1 Allergic reactions
1.1.2 Secondary pharmacological actions	2.1.2 Anaphylaxis
1.1.3 Rebound response on discontinuation of drug	2.2 Idiosyncracy
	2.3 Genetically determined effects.

1. **Predictable ADR**

   All the drugs have many pharmacological actions or effects on different systems or system organs; but the physician takes in account only one effect at a therapeutic dose. Such ADR basically results due to a quantitative drug intolerence which includes other effects such as.

   1.1 **Other effects :** It is a result of use of excess dose of drug, use of OTC or self medication and in some cases due to discontinuation of drug during a therapy. These effects are summarisd below.

   1.1.1 **Excessive Pharmacological actions :** It is very common with drugs like tranquillizers, sedatives and hypnotics and anti-epileptics. On the administration of such drugs in high dose can be dangerous to the patient. Even at average dose some individuals are susceptible showing reactions due to Kidney, Hepatic disfunctioning or alteration in pharmacokinetic pattern.

   1.1.2 **Secondary Pharmacological actions :** It is mainly observed in patients, who consume OTC drugs or go for self medication. e.g. Drugs like antihistamics used mainly as anti-allergic particularly for common cold and cough may produce drowziness in large or repeated doses on self-medication.

   1.1.3 **Rebound response on dicontinuation of drug :** In case of psychotropic drugs and Narcotic analgesics rebound responses either psychological or physical withdrawal symptoms occur.

2. **Unpredictable Adverse drug reactions :**

   When the drug is given in an average dose or very small dose hypersensitivity reactions may occur. These include the following types.

   2.1 **Qualitative intolerance :** Intolerance to the drug by the individual shows because of immune responses of body or lacking of enzyme activity which results into hyper responses, such as :

   2.1.1 **Allergic reactions :** They are also called hypersensitivity reactions. The word allergy is derived from a greek word i.e.

   Allos : means Altered

   Ergos : means Energy

   These are common reactions resulting when the drug acts as an antigen, which then reacts with either autocoids like histamine, serotonin or bradykinin to produce allergic reactions like skin rashes, reddening of skin with itching or sometimes autoimmune mechanism of body produces antibodies usually IgG and IgM to block the antigen (drug), called antigen, antibody reactions result into precipitation or Agglutination etc. and this may cause hypersensitivity reactions.

e.g. • Sulpha and barbiturates produces skin rashes.

• Quinidine and methyl-dopa causes haemolytic anemias.

2.1.2 Anaphylaxis : It is the major form of allergic or hypersensitivity reactions occuring mainly due to activity of IgE antibody. It is characterised by pulmonary and circulatory collapse as asthma and hypotension respectively. Skin rashes may result with localised edema.

e.g. Penicillin and Plasma expanders like Dextrans 40 or 60.

2.2 Idiosyncrasy : A Greek word "idos - one's own" and "synkrasis - together". It is also a qualitative type of drug intolerance, but occurs in other than auto-immune mechanism of body. The mechanism may be known in few cases e.g. The reactions shown by the individuals to a group or a specific drug like antimalerials, antibiotics, hormones, sulpha, salicylates and furan compounds because of reduced or lacking of enzyme activity such as Glucose-6-phosphate dehydrogenase causes haemolysis. Hormones (oestrogen) produces cancer to uterus.

2.3 Genetically determined effects : The drug produces toxic effects because of individual variations or hereditary disorders; the metabolism pathway in liver is altered, those patients of selected genetic characters are susceptible for specific drugs. e.g. Isoniazide.

Reasons for Adverse Drug Reactions

1. **Medication errors :**

    (a) Self-medication of OTC drugs by patient leads to over use or misuse of drug. It may result into excess pharmacological action or complications.

    (b) Over-prescribing of potent medicament to the patient e.g. oral hypoglycemic, antihypertensives etc.

2. **Inadequate monitoring of the patient :** Drugs like cardiotonics, Diuretics, corticosteroids needs therapeutic monitoring with continuing the administration beyond therapeutic end point which leads into adverse reactions.

3. **Sudden withdrawal of drugs :** Therapy with drugs like carticosteroids and hormones can not be suddenly stopped. Such drugs therapy is gradually stopped by decreasing the dose.

4. **Bio-availability variations :** There are number of brands of the same drug manufactured by different companies with varying manufacturing process which leads to variations in bio-availability of drugs.

5. **New potent drugs :** The ever increasing number of new potent drugs, along with brands, may cause hypersensitivity reactions in particular individuals.

6. **Drug interaction and drug food interaction :** This phenomenon may produce adverse effect. It has been explained in detailed in the previous chapter.

7. **Patient factor :**
   (a) **Idiosyncracy of Individual :** Refer 2.2.
   (b) **Age :** Young and old patients are more susceptible to adverse drug reactions as compared to the adults, because of pharmacokinetic pattern at this age.
   (c) **Disease state :** Mainly patients with hepatic or renal disfunctioning are prone to adverse effect of drugs.
   (d) **Discontinuation of therapy/treatment due to :**
      (i) high cost of medicine.
      (ii) lack of faith on physician.
      (iii) Non-compliance.

Kinds of Drug - Induced Diseases :

Apart from the therapeutic action of drug it may act on different systems or organs as well. This characteristic of drug can induce disease condition as discussed below :

I. Drug -induced Gastro intestinal disorders :

Oral route of administration for a drug is very common. In a single prescription almost 80% of drugs are in oral form, therefore there is great possibility of GIT disorders. They are summarised in the table :

Adverse Drug Reaction	Example of Drugs
1. Nausea and Vomitting	Most of the drugs given orally.
2. Dysgensia (change in taste)	Antibiotics, Bitters, Alkaloids and Metronidazole.
3. Constipation	Haematinics, Nortryptiline, Verapramil, Ephedrine, Morphine.
4. Diarrhoea	Ampicillin, Neomycin, Cardiotonics and Atropine.
5. Ulceration	Salicylates, NSAID and Sulpha.

II. Drug Induced Liver Disorders :

Drugs are metabolised and excreted at liver site. It is commonly affected by drugs. About 10% of drugs may cause jaundice and acute hepatitis. The hepatotoxic drugs are categorised into two types :

(a) Drugs causing direct liver damage : Because of some specific chemical structure and properties, they may alter or cause interference in metabolism. e.g. Isoniazide, tetracycline, methotrexate aspirin, cemetidine.

(b) Drugs causing damage to liver by host hypersensitivity : e.g. Sulphonamides, Erythromycin, MAO inhibitors phenytoin. These drugs cause allergic reactions such as rash, fever, eosinophillia.

III. Drug Induced Renal Disorders :

Kidney is a perfused organ, highly sensitive to the effects of drugs as compared to other organs. The renal cells are exposed to drug concentration in pyramids of medula, causing toxic effects.

pH of urine causes precipitation of some drugs. The antigen antibody complexes get deposited on endothelial lining of kidney, which may cause hypersensitivity reactions.

Type of Nephrotoxicity	Examples of drug
1. Direct damage to glomerular or renal tubules.	Cephalosporin, Polymixin, Aminoglycosides, Cyclosporin A, Organic iodides.
2. Diabetes – insipidus	Lithium, sulphonylureas methoxyflurane
3. Kidney stone Renal calculi	Sulphonamides
4. Nephritis	NSAID, diuretics, synthetic penicillin.

IV. Drug - Induced Haematological disorders :

Haemopoietic system and functioning of the bone marrow may be affected by some drugs, thereby disturbing components of the blood. The common disorders are anaemias, leukopenia, thrombocytopenia.

Disorder	Examples of drug
1. Anaemias	
(a) Aplastic	Chloramphenicol, Phenylbutazone, Oxyphenbutazone
(b) Megaloblastic	Isoniazide, purine, phenytoin.
(c) Haemolytic	Antimalarials, antibacterials analgesics.
2. Leukopenia	Sulphonamides, Antithyroid drugs
3. Thrombocytopenia	Aspirin, ibuprofen, penicillin heparin and alcohol.

V. Drug - Induced Dermatological reactions

These are mainly photosensitive type of reactions which take place between the drug or its metabolite and U.V. rays. The reactions may be **phototoxic** or **photoallergic**.

Phototoxic reactions are dose related effect resulting after first exposure of drug. Are characterised by conditions resembling to sunburns. e.g. Tetracycline, Hexachlorophene.

Photoallergic reactions are produced by antigen formed by the effect of light on the drug and skin proteins. It is characterised by eczematous eruption e.g. Thiazides, antihistamines, oestrogens.

VI. Teratogenicity :

Teros means **monster**. Administration of a few drugs during pregnancy results in birth of monster-like baby. Teratogenecity term is applied to undesized harmful effects of a drug on the foetus , when the drug is given to the mother during pregnancy.

The reasons for teratogenicity are attributed to chemical nature of drug and to the placental barrier which exposes foetus to almost all the drugs that are administered to the mother.

Drug or chemical agent that effects abnormalities in developing embryo are called **"Teratogens"**. Teratogens act by two ways :

1. **Act directly on the foetus :** During the organogenesis phase i.e. first 16 - 58 days of developing embryo, drugs like Thalidomide and methotrexate, androgen act directly on the foetus, by affecting the cell division, protein synthesis and DNA synthesis.

2. **Act indirectly :**
   (a) **On the placenta :** Vit. A and its several analogs, after the normal processes; leads to deficiency of critical substances appears to play a role in some types of abnormalities.
   (b) **On the Uterus :** Vasoconstrictor act on the uterus by reducing the blood supply and causes foetal anoxia.
   (c) **On the mother hormone balance :** Hormones such as androgens and progesterone may affect the hormone balance of a mother and causes foetal distress.

The teratogenesity is classified on the basis of abnormality occurs in a new born babies.

1. **Structural teratogenesity :** Teratogens produces various abnormalities according to the stage of gestation period of first 10 – 12 week. It includes different stages.

    (a) **Pre-Implementation :** 12 days from conception to implantation. Exposure to teratogen can kill embryo.

    (b) **Period of organogenesis :** 13 - 56 days a and b forms together **first trimester**. In this malformation or abortion (miscarriage) may result.

    (c) **The II and III trimester :** In this stage there is growth and development of teeth, bone, CNS and endocrine system. Exposure to harmful drugs can cause a variety of post-natal effects such as retardation of physical or brain growth.

    (d) **Short labour - delivery stage :** In this stage paralysis in new born babies is seen.

2. **Behavioural teratogenesity :** Apart from the structural abnormalities, a teratogen can cause psychological abnormalities in a new born. This is found in new borns of mothers who are exposed to **methyl mercury** by eating contaminated food and smoke during pregnancy.

Sr. No.	Teratogen	Nature of Teratogenesity
1.	Thalidomide	Structural teratogenesity (Affected limbs are observed)
2.	Methyl mercury	Behavioural teratogenisity (psychological abnormalities are seen)

Role of a Pharmacist in Adverse drug reactions :

There is a limited scope to the pharmacist in performing clinical studies or toxicity studies; but he can collect the information from patients medical history, which will be helpful to him at the time of patients advices, counselling and therapeutic monitoring. The pharmacist must consider the following factors :

1. **Interactions of Drug-Drug :** e.g. A diabetic patient taking phenylbutazone (NSAID) there will be an increased hypoglycemic effect. So, the phamacist avoid giving this drug to the patient.

2. **Interactions of Drug-food :** e.g. Patient taking tetracycline with milk or food containing calcium should be avoided.

3. **Disease condition of patient :** Patient suffering from GIT disfunction or disorders like vomitting/diarrhoea; oral drugs cannot be prescribed.

4. **Genetically determined factors** : Refer Article 2.2 and 2.3 unpredictable reactions.

5. **The pharmacist** can monitor the patients compliance during therapy, such as hormonal, psychiatric, which on discontinuation produces withdrawal symptoms.

QUESTIONS

1. Define ADR and classify ADR.   **[S - 03, 97, W - 00) 4 marks]**
2. What is adverse drug reaction ?   **[W - 97) 4 marks]**
3. What are unpredictable reactions ?   **[W - 97) 4 marks]**
4. What is idiosyncrasy ?   **[(S - 96, W - 01, 97) 4 marks]**
5. Give various reasons of adverse drug reactions ? How they are prevented.
      [(S - 96 : W - 02, 97) 4 marks]
6. What is drug induced GIT toxicity ? Explain with suitable examples.
      [(S - 99) 4 marks]
7. Explain with examples, drug induced dermatological reactions.
      [(W - 99) 4 marks]
8. Write note on Teratogenisity.
      [(S - 03, 01, 00, 96 : W - 03, 02, 99, 97) 4 marks]
9. Discuss the role of a pharmacist in preventing ADR.   **[(W - 01) 4 marks]**

■■■

8
DRUGS IN CLINICAL TOXICITY

(You the evil, I the cure)

INTRODUCTION

Almost all the chemical substances or drugs in toxic dose may be poison and a poison in small dose can be a medicine. There is really no boundary between medicine and poison.

A poison can be **defined** as a chemical substance which, when administered, inhaled or swallowed is capable of producing lethal effect on the body.

In law a substance given for a purpose of life saving is medicine and to produce harm to the body is poison. These are governed by the **"Poison Act 1919"**. The Maharashtra State Government framed the rules and regulations under **"Maharashtra Poison Act 1972"**, which includes a schedule "e" giving a list of poisons as :

1. **Class A poisons** : Generally are those used as medicine. e.g. Atropine salt, Aconite salt, Opium derivatives, Digitalis glycosides etc.
2. **Class B poisons** : They do not have any medicinal use e.g. Oxides of mercury, Arsenic salt, Strychnine phenols etc.

Gravity of poisoning :

There are two types :

1. **Acute poisoning** : In such toxicity the symptoms of poisoning appears suddenly after injection or administration of poison; which rapidly increases severity and followed by death or recovery.
2. **Chronic poisoning** : Symptoms develop gradually over a time of period like malase.

Difference between Acute and Chronic Poisoning :

Acute Poisoning	Chronic Poisoning
1. Sudden appearance of signs and symptoms.	Gradual persistence of symptoms.
2. Characterised by affected respiration, blood pressure and unconsciousness etc.	Loss of appetite, body weight, muscular weakness and malase etc.
3. Withdrawal symptoms do not occur.	Withdrawal complications are very common.
4. Specific antagonists with general measures are employed.	Antagonists with rehabilitation and treatment of withdrawal symptoms are done.
5. e.g. Heavy metal, insecticide.	e.g. Narcotics, Barbiturates etc.

Classification of Poisons :

No classification of poison is purely satisfactory, but they are generally classified on the basis of mode of actions ; and are classified into "six" groups.

1. **Corrosive poisons :** They produce inflammation and acute ulceration of tissues. The symptoms are pain in throat and stomach with odour of acid.

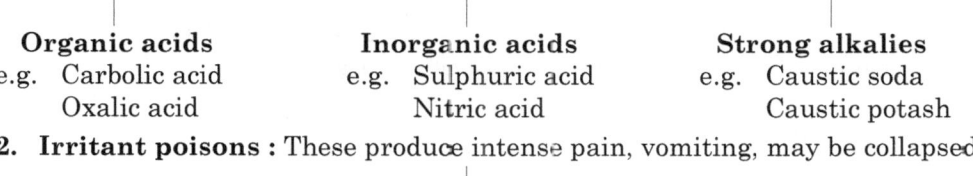

	Organic acids	**Inorganic acids**	**Strong alkalies**
e.g.	Carbolic acid	e.g. Sulphuric acid	e.g. Caustic soda
	Oxalic acid	Nitric acid	Caustic potash

2. **Irritant poisons :** These produce intense pain, vomiting, may be collapsed.

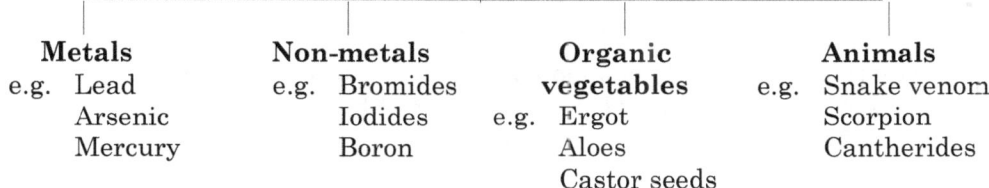

	Metals	**Non-metals**	**Organic vegetables**	**Animals**
e.g.	Lead	e.g. Bromides	e.g. Ergot	e.g. Snake venom
	Arsenic	Iodides	Aloes	Scorpion
	Mercury	Boron	Castor seeds	Cantherides

3. **Neurotic poisons :** These act on CNS, producing headache, drowsiness, giddiness, stupor, coma etc.

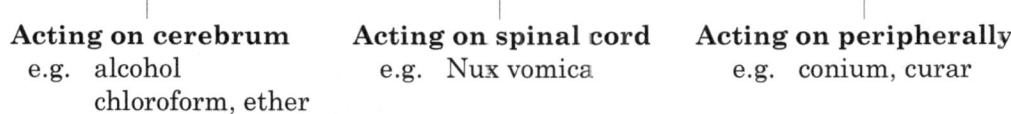

Acting on cerebrum	**Acting on spinal cord**	**Acting on peripherally**
e.g. alcohol	e.g. Nux vomica	e.g. conium, curar
chloroform, ether		

4. **Cardiac poisons :** Poisons act particularly on the heart producing deterious effect. e.g. Aconite, Oleander, Quinine etc.

5. **Asphyxiants :** Act on lungs only e.g. carbonmonoxide, carbon dioxide, coal gases etc.

6. **Miscellaneous :** It includes numerous category drugs, which are capable of producing the toxic effects e.g phenacetin, tranquilizers. Lysergic acid derivatives etc.

General treatment of Poisoning :

Poison in relatively small amounts may cause structural damage or functional disturbances in the body. Poisoning can be accidental, suicidal or homicidal. The victim needs immediate treatment. It involves the following measures :

1. Immediate care of deteriorating body functions.
2. Removal of unabsorbed poison.
3. Elimination of absorbed poison.
4. Use of Antidotes.
5. Supportive measures.

1. **Immediate care of deteriorating body functions**

   It totally depends on the condition of patient; but certain measures that are commonly essential are :

   (a) Keeping air way patent by artificial respiration.

   (b) Care of blood circulation by treatment of hypotension.

2. **Removal of unabsorbed poison**

   (a) Prevention of further exposure, in case of poison absorbed through skin or inhaled by shifting the patient from that atmosphere.

   (b) Emesis : Syrups like Ipecac are effective in the first 2 hours, produce stimulation of pharynx resulting in emesis.

   (c) Adsorbents : Activated charcoal, 10-40 gm in water is given. It adsorbs almost all the poisons but it is not given with Ipecac.

   (d) Gastric lavage : It is adopted in case of unconscious patients, when the poison is injested by GIT can be removed by washing stomach with saline solution or water to remove unabsorbed poison.

3. **Elimination of absorbed poison**

   Elimination rate may be enhanced by giving saline cathetors like $MgSO_4$ or sorbitol OR The urine is made either acidic or basic in case of basic drugs (e.g. amphetamin) and acidic drugs respectively.

4. **Use of Antidotes :**

   Antidotes are the substances which antagonise the effect of toxicants, specifically or non-specifically. They are classified mainly into three groups :

   (i) Non-systemic antidotes

   (ii) Systemic antidotes

   (iii) Universal antidotes.

   (i) Non-systemic antidotes : These are mostly given after emesis by oral route. And are further sub-divided on the basis of how they act.

       (a) Mechanical antidotes : These are substances which prevent further absorption of poison. They act by forming a coat over mucous membrane of stomach. e.g. oils, fats and egg albumin etc.

       (b) Chemical antidotes : These react by chemical means with poison and neutralise their toxic effect. e.g. magnesium oxide, calcium oxide and tannins etc.

   (ii) Systemic antidotes : Such substances produce the opposite actions of effect to that of poison. These are administered with care because the antagonism always not complete, the antidote itself may produce unwanted effects. e.g. BAL (Dimercaprol), EDTA salts etc.

(a) Dimecaprol (BAL) : Dimercaprol commonly known as BAL i.e. **"British Anti Lewisite"**. It is a chelating agent with sulfhydryl group, form a non-toxic water soluble complex with Arsenic, antimony, gold etc. It not only prevents the enzymatic inhibition produced by heavy metals but also reactivates them. An overdose of BAL is administered because of the only problem that the formed complex may dissociate, which liberates metal ions; then these again react with excess drug.

Indications :

(a) **Arsenic, mercury, antimony poisoning**

Dose : Arsenic poisoning – 3 mg/kg IM every 4 hours mercury poisoning - 5 mg/kg followed 2.5 mg/kg IM BD for 10 days.

Lead poisoning : 4 mg/kg IM every 4 hours for 2 days and then every 6 hours for 2 days and then every 12 hours for 7 days.

Adverse effects :
- rise in blood pressure
- tachycardia (increase in heart rate)
- nausia, vomiting and headache
- burning sensation in oral cavity, etc.

Uses : It is used as a antidote in Arsenic, lead and mercury poisoning.

(b) Di-sodium EDTA (Edetate)

It is called chelating agent. This is a sodium salt of ethylene diamine tetra acetate. It forms water soluble non-toxic complex with divalent and tetravalent metallic ions. It is given by the injectable route.

Dose :

- For diagnosis of lead poisoning : 70 – 75 mg/kg in 3 divided doses.
- For treatment : 40 mg/kg/day in 2 doses by I.M. for 5 days.
  200 mg/ml of I.V. with 5% Dextrose or Normal saline.
  Total amount not be exceed 500 mg/kg during therapy.

Uses :

(i) For diagnosis of poisoning like lead.
(ii) As a antidote in lead and mercury poisoning.
(iii) In condition of hypercalcemia due to affinity with calcium ion.

(c) Penicillamine :

Penicillamine can be given by oral route. It forms non-toxic water soluble complex with copper, mercury lead etc. It has immunological properties with an ability to reduce IgM rheumatoid factor and hence supresses the disease.

Dose :
- In poisoning : 0.5 - 1.5 g/day in 4 divided doses.
- In Wilson's disease : 1 - 5 gm/day in divided doses, depending on condition.
- In Rheumatoid arthritis : 125 - 750 mg/day.

Uses :
(i) As a antidote in lead, copper, mercury poisoning etc.
(ii) In treatment of Wilson's disease (characteristics by abnormal metabolism of copper and so copper deposited in liver and brain due to hepatolenticular degeneration).
(iii) In a treatment of rheumatoid arthritis.
(iv) In a treatment of chronic active hepatitis.

(d) Desferrioxamine :

Mostly it binds with ferric ions to form non-toxic water soluble complex that are eliminated via urine and bile. Iron from hemosiderin is also removed by desferrioxamine.

Doses :
- In acute cases :
  * 2 gm/lit. for gastric leavage.
  * 1 gm immediately and followed 0.5 gm every 4 hrs. for 2 days.
  * Then 500 mg every 4-12 hours.

The total amount not to exceed 6 gm/day.

- In chronic cases :
  * 0.5 to 1 gm by I.M.
  * 1-2 gm by sub-cutaneous route.

Uses :
(i) As an antidote in acute and chronic iron poisoning.

(iii) Universal Antidotes : It is used where the nature of poison is unknown. This is a mixture of three ingredients given in a dose of tablespoonful, repeated twice or thrice.

The composition is given below :

Constituents	Quantity	Purpose
1. Powdered charcoal (burnt toast)	2 parts	Absorbs alkaloid
2. Magnesium oxide (milk of magnesia)	1 part	Neutralise acids
3. Tannic acid (strong tea)	1 part	Precipitates alkaloids certain glycosides and many metals

Uses :

(i) Universal antidote is used in the poisoning of - Alkaloids like datura because of charcoal and tannic acid.

(ii) Glycoside and metallic poisoning can be precipitated by the presence of tannic acid.

(iii) In acidic poisoning universal antidote is given which is neutralised by milk of magnesia.

5. Supportive Measures :

The patient is kept warm and comfortable by treating other symptoms mentioned in the following table :

Symptom	Therapy
Dehydration	Normal saline injection
Glucose level depletion	Dextrose infusion
CNS related	Anticonvulsants
CVS related	Antiarrhythmics
Pain	Analgesics

INSECTICIDES POISONING

Many of the insecticides contains :

(A) Organophosphorus compounds like marathion, tetraethyl pyrophosphate hexaethyl tetra phosphate etc.

(B) DDT

(C) Endrine

Symptoms :

These includes :
- Headache
- Irritation of eyes, nose and throat
- Blurring vision
- Cough followed by vomiting with abdominal pain.
- In severe cases salivation, nervousness and convulsions may occur.
- If not attended in time respiratory failure, coma and finally death may occur.

Treatment :

Treatment involves the following steps :

- **(a) Decontamination :** The victim is removed from the source of contamination from further exposure. Washing of skin by water with soap is done.
- **(b) Emesis :** Vomiting is induced if poison is ingested by giving tincture of ipecac.
- **(c) Gastric lavage :** In case of severe condition of patient it is carried to remove unabsorbed poison.
- **(d) Antidotes :** Specific antidote given to block their effects are given in the table :

Poison	Antidote	Dose
(i) Organophosphorous compounds	Atropine (patient shall be fully atropinised)	2 mg every 15 – 30 min. by IM or IV.
(ii) D.D.T.	Phenobarbitone	100 mg orally every 4 to 6 hours.
(iii) Endrine	10% calcium lactate	10 ml by I.V. every 4 to 6 hours.

Simultaneously "artificial respiration" is essential in serious condition of the patient.

- **(e) Use of choline esterase reactivator :** Atropine can block the peripheral actions, particularly of organophosphorous compounds but not produced on CNS like convulsions and neuromuscular cramps. Such effects are neutralised by giving choline - esterase reactivator as 5% strength in **Normal Saline drip.**

    e.g.
    - PAM (Pyridine aldoxy methionate)
    - Pralidoxine chloride or iodide

    In dose of 1 – 2 gm by I.V. for adults and 30 - 50 mg/kg for children at every 12 hours.

- **(f) Other care :** Apart from symptomatic treatment of headache, abdominal pain etc. Mercurial diuretics and barbitone can be given.

HEAVY METAL POISONING

There are few metals, that cause poisonous effect in our body; such as arsenic, lead, mercury antimony etc. The gravity of effect may be acute or chronic poisoning. The symptoms and treatment is as under :

- **(A) Arsenic Poisoning :** Arsenic is found in air, soil and well water etc. Smelting process of copper and lead releases arsenic into the environment. It looks like sugar, cheap and easily available in market.

1. **Acute arsenic poisoning :** A specific form of arsenic i.e. AS_2O_3 (Arsenic tri-oxide) that is readily available and has appearance of sugar. Though it is rare, but responsible for acute poisoning.

   Symptoms :
   - Gastro intestinal tract discomfort.
   - Burning pain of lips, stomach etc.
   - Vomiting with stomach content followed by greenish and blackish mucous fluid.
   - Vomiting later on followed by diarrhoea.
   - Muscular cramps and convulsions.
   - Visual disturbances etc.

   Treatment :
   - Gastric lavage with warm water.
   - Emetics like mustard and zinc sulphate are used.
   - Freshly prepared hydrated ferric oxide is introduced in stomach as an antidote, which converts arsenious acid in non-toxic formic arsinate.
   - Dimercaprol (BAL) 2.5 – 3 mg/kg every 4 hours by I.M. for 2 days, every 6 hours for 10 days and every 12 hours till symptoms disappear.

   OR
   - Penicillamine 0.5 – 1.5 gm/day in 4 divided dosage with meal in the treatment of choice for 1 week.
   - Morphine can be used to abolish pain.

2. **Chronic arsenic poisoning :** Chronic poisoning consists of a number stages of symptoms may result after :

   (i) acute attack

   (ii) accidental consumption of small doses, either in drinks or food.

   Symptoms :

   (a) **Stage of GIT disturbances :** It includes :
   - Nausea
   - Loss of appetite and malnutrition
   - Loss of body weight

   (b) **Stage of catarrhal changes :** means inflammation to mucous membrane, especially of nose.
   - Running of eyes and nose
   - Inflammation to mucous membrane causes conjuctivitis.
   - Coughing because of bronchial inflammation.

   (c) **Skin Rashes :**
   - There are brown patchy pigmentation of skin, particularly on neck region.
   - Nails become brittle.

- Shedding of hairs.
- Hyperkeratosis of palms and soles.
- Irritation to the skin occurs with vesicular erruption.

(d) Nervous disturbances :
- Muscular fatigue and weakness.
- Numbness of hands, feets and fingers.
- Convulsions.
- Impaired vision etc.

Treatment :
- Removal of victim from further exposure.
- Sodium thiosulphate - 1 gm in 10 ml SWFI, 2-3 times per week for couple of months by I.V. route.
- Dimercaprol 3 mg/kg every 6 hours by a week and every 12 hours for several weeks by I.M. route.

(B) Lead Poisoning : Lead poisoning usually is by oral, respiratory or cutaneous route. Colour paints, glass and petroleum industries use lead. Children play with toys and suck them. Fumes resulting from glass and petrol burning are inhaled. Lead is accumulated in RBC, Liver, Kidney and Bones. Acute poisoning is rare.

1. Acute Poisoning : It occurs very rare, the homocidal and suicidal cases are not seen.

Symptoms :
- metallic taste
- muscle cramps
- stools become black
- haemolytic crisis may result
- general weakness etc.

Treatment :
- Gastric lavage by sodium or magnesium sulphate.
- Calcium EDTA 200 mg/ml in 5% Dextrose or Normal Saline injection is administered by IV.
  OR
  30 – 50 mg/kg/day in 2 divided doses by IM route for 5 days is given.
  The total amount of Ca-EDTA should not exceed 500 mg/kg during the treatment.
- Purgative may be given alongwith antispasmodic.
- As per need barbiturates and manitol is given.

2. Chronic poisoning : It is commonly known as "plumbism". Chronic lead poisoning is done over a prolonged period of time. Mainly it is seen in children playing with them or in workers of printing and petroleum industries.

Symptoms :
- **General symptoms** like metallic taste, constipation and cramps.
- **Lead line :** Bluish black lines are observed on gingival margins.
- **Anaemia :** Microcytic hypochromic type of anaemia with punctuate basophillia.
- **Lead palsy :** It is characterised by muscle weakness.
- **Lead encephalopathy :** The cerebral (CNS) symptoms are known as lead encephalopathy and characterised as :
  * headache and sleeplessness (Hyposomnia)
  * restlessness and irritability
  * tremors of fingers, face and eyes
  * delirium and finally convulsions etc.

Treatment :
- Removal of victim from further exposure.
- Excretion of accumulated lead in the body can be facilitated by acidosis.
- Ca - EDTA used as in acute poisoning.
- Dimercaprol (BAL) is also given with edetate in a dose of 4 mg/kg every 4 to 6 hours by I.M. route.
- Symptomatic treatment includes use of anticonvulsants antispasmodics or mannitol to reduce intracranial tension.

(B) Mercury Poisoning : Environmental pollution is the source of mercury poisoning. Workers working in minor, thermometer, barometer and electrical industries are exposed to this poisoning.

1. Acute Poisoning : The symptoms includes :

Symptoms :
- metallic taste in mouth.
- Inflammation of gingival.
- White coating on tongue.
- Burning pain in GIT.
- Hematuria and albuminuria.
- Cardice arrhythmias.
- Convulsions etc.

Treatment :
- Gastric lavage and artificial respiration.
- Charcoal, egg to prevent further absorption.
- Dimercaprol 300 mg by IM immediately and 150 mg two times for 2-3 days.
- Alternatively penicillumine may be used.

Chronic poisoning : Contaminated diet of fish is the major source of chronic mercury poisoning.

Symptoms :
- Excessive salivation with inflammation of salivary glands.
- Brownish blue lines on gums with loosen teeth.
- GIT disturbances.
- Tremors of tongue and fingers.

Treatment :
- Removal of patient from exposure.
- Enhancement of mercury excretion via kidney.
- Dimercaprol as an antidote.
- Use of anti-cholinergic (belladonna dry extract) 30-40 mg in three doses to reduce excessive salivation.

BARBITURATE POISONING

These compounds are mainly used as sedatives and hypnotics. They were also used as anti-psychotics, anti-epileptics.

Symptoms :
- May cause excitement.
- Restlessness and mental confusion.
- Slowed speech and delirium.
- Respiratory depression.
- Hypotension and muscular weakness.
- Coma, finally death due to respiratory failure.

Treatment :
- Gastric lavage by using potassium permanganate solution or a suspension of charcoal.
- Hypertensive like metarminol in a dose of 2.5 mg by I.V. may be given.
- Use of Analeptics which stimulate CNS.
- Use of forced osmotic diuretics like manitol 20% of 500 ml solution.

NARCOTIC POISONING

This group of poisons are also known as somniferous. Their preparations are used therapeutically to reduce pain and produce sleep. The main poisons in this group are opium and pithidine.

Opium is obtained by incision of the unripe fruit of poppy plant called "papaver somniferum".

Symptoms : The symptoms of opium poisoning can be categorised in the following stages :

(a) Stage of excitement : Initially well-being and comfort with pleasurable mental excitement, lasts for very short duration. Euphoria, Laughter with increased heart rate.

(b) Stage of sopor : The stage of excitement is followed headache, giddiness, a sense of weight in limbs, strong tendency to sleep etc.

(c) Stage of Narcosis :
- Patient goes into deep coma.
- Muscles are relaxed and reflex are abolished.
- Pupil are contracted, but do not respond to light.
- Blood pressure falls.

Treatment :
- Gastric lavage with water and potassium permanganate solution in ratio of 1 : 1000.
- Purgatives like magnesium sulphate 15 ml orally can be given.
- 1.5 mg Atropine can be useful.
- Artificial respiration may be given.

Role of Pharmacist in Clinical Toxicity

The pharmacist does not directly involved in the therapy of poisoning except for first aid. He plays a key role in ensuring that adequate information and equipment are available.

Apart from this in few poisoning cases he can reduce further toxication of poison by adopting the measures of general treatment is as follows :

Animal Poisoning: Particularly in case of snake poisoning he may function as :
- Alloying anxiety and freight that all snakes are not poisonous.
- Application of torniquets to prevent further spread of poison.
- Application of ice cubes at site of bite.
- Immediate hospitalisation of victim.

Insecticide poisoning :
- Washing of hands and skin areas which are exposed.
- Removal of clothes.
- Emesis and Immediate hospitalization.

List of antidotes :

Sr. No.	Category of Poison	Antidote
(A)	**Organic acids and bases :**	
(i)	Sulphuric acid (oil of vitriol)	Milk of magnesia (orally)
(ii)	Hydrochloric acid	
(iii)	Nitric acid	
(iv)	Caustic potash and Soda	Vinegar, lemon or orange juice
(B)	**Organic acids :**	
(i)	Oxalic acid (acid of sugar)	Calcium gluconate
(ii)	Carbolic acid (phenol)	Sodium sulphate and alkaline saline by I.V.
(iii)	Salicylic acid	Sodium bi-carbonate, magnesium oxide.
(C)	**Vegetable acids :**	
(i)	Hydrocynic acid	Sodium thiosulphate injection, dicobalt tetracemate injection.
(D)	**Vegetable Poison :**	
(i)	Castor oil	No specific, but I.V. glucose and saline.
(ii)	Ergot	Nicotinamide and vasodilator.
(E)	**Miscellaneous :**	
(i)	Opium and Morphine	Nalorphine (0.4 to 0.8 mg I.V.), Amiphenazole (30 mg I.V.)
(ii)	Pithidine	Coramine
(iii)	LSD	Ca-gluconate
(iv)	Alcohol	vitamin B-6 (50 - 100 mg I.V.), Coramine (3 - 5 ml I.V.)
(v)	Barbiturate	Coramine (5 mg I.V.), Analeptics
(vi)	Nicotine	1.5% Atropine - SO_4.
(vii)	Aspirin	vitamin K_1
(viii)	Paracetamol	Cysteamine (200 mg I.V.)
(ix)	Amphetamine	Sedative with chlorpromazine
(x)	Anti-depressants	Physostigmine (2 - 4 mg% I.V.)
(xi)	Antihistaminics	Diazepam (10 - 20 mg I.V.)
(xii)	Dhatura	Neostigmine and Physotigmine
(xiii)	Digitalis	Atropine and tri-sodium EDTA.
(xiv)	D.D.T.	Atropine (I.V.)

Contd. ...

(xv)	Physostigmine	Atropine
(xvi)	Pentazocine	Naloxone (5 mg/kg I.V.)
(xvii)	Atropine	Physostigmine (0.5 - 2 mg I.V.)
(xviii)	Benzodiazepines e.g. Diazepam	Flumazenil (2.5 - 10 mg I.V.)
(xix)	Organophosphorous	Atropine (2 mg I.V.), Pralidoxime (1 - 2 mg I.V.)
(xx)	Strychnine	Diazepam (I.V.)
(xxi)	Ethylene glycol	Ethanol by I.V. Adult : 0.69 g/kg - 7 to 10 g over 1 hr. Child : 0.6 g/kg - 4.5 g over 1 hr. Methylene blue : 1% solution by I.V.
(F)	**Metals :**	
(i)	Antimony	BAL - 3 mg/kg body wt. 4 times on 1st day followed by thrice for 10 days
(ii)	Arsenic	BAL
(iii)	Copper	Cuprimine, Penicillamine
(iv)	Iron	Desferioxamine
(v)	Lead	Na - EDTA, Penicillamine

QUESTIONS

1. Define Poison. Differentiate acute and chronic poisoning.
   [(S - 04, 93, 92, 98) 4 marks]
2. Classify poison with examples. [(W - 03, 01, 00, 98, 97 : S - 97) 4 marks]
3. Write short note on BAL. [W - 96]
4. Write short note EDTA. [W - 96]
5. Give the composition of universal antidotes and give its uses.
   [(S - 02, 01, 96) 3 marks]

   OR

6. Universal antidotes in the treatment of poisoning. [S - 00]
7. Write short note on Insecticide OR organophosphorous poisoning.
   [(S - 02, 97, 96 : W - 01, 00, 98) 4 marks]
8. How is arsenic poisoning treated ? [(S - 99, W - 00)]
9. What is acute poisoning ? How lead poisoning is treated ? [(W - 99) 4 mark]
10. Heavy metal poisoning. [(S - 03, 00, 99 : W - 99) 4 marks]

■■■

9

DRUG DEPENDENCE

(The Mercy)

INTRODUCTION

Every society has a trend of use of drug that alters mood, pleasures, feelings, attitude and behaviour. When they are repeatedly consumed it leads to habit or addiction so called dependence.

1. **Drug Abuse :** It is defined as the consumption of a drug apart from medical need or in excess quantities or not for medical purpose of any drug to experience it's pleasurable effects.
2. **Drug Addiction :** It is a state of chronic or periodic intoxication resulting from repeated consumption of drug.
3. **Drug Habituation :** It is a state resulting from the repeated use of drug.
4. **Drug Tolerance :** It is a condition in which a decreased therapeutic response of a drug or related drug effect shown by an individual.
5. **Drug Dependence :** The World Heath Organization has defined it as, a state, psychic and some times physical in which the user has a compelling desire to continue taking the drug either to experience its effect or to avoid the discomfort of its absence.

Difference between Drug Addiction and Drug Habituation :

Drug Addiction	Drug Habituation.
1. It is a state of chronic or periodic intoxication due to repeated consumption of drug.	It is a state resulting from the repeated use of drug.
2. A compulsion to continue taking the drug or overpowering desire.	A desire but not compulsion to continue taking the drug to improve a sense of well-being
3. A tendency to increase a dose of drug.	Little or no tendency to increase of dose.
4. A psychic, particularly physical, dependence shown by the individual on the effects of the drug.	Some degree of psychic dependence but none of physical dependence shown by an individual.
5. Withdrawal symptoms are observed.	Little or No withdrawal symptoms are there.
e.g. Morphine, Heroin, Alcohol, LSD and its derivatives etc.	e.g. Tea, Coffee etc.

Differences between psychological and physical drug dependence :

Psychologic drug dependence	Physical drug dependence
1. It is a state characterized by an emotional or mental desire to continue taking a drug.	It is a state which shows itself by intense physical disturbances in case the drug is not administered.
2. No compulsion to take the drug.	There is compulsion to take the drug.
3. Withdrawal symptoms are not observed or very minor.	Withdrawal or abstinence symptoms are observed.
4. No need of specific drug to treat withdrawal symptoms in case of any.	Specific antagonist with supportive therapy is needed.
5. e.g. Nicotine, caffeine	e.g. Opiates, alcohol.

Treatment of drug abuse :

The treatment aspects of drug abuse are as follows :

(i) Detoxification.

(ii) Care of withdrawal symptoms.

(iii) Rehabilitation.

(iv) Govt. Support.

(i) **Detoxification :** Firstly the adverse effects result from drug abuse with a specific drug are treated by hospitalising the patient. The use of such drugs are stopped immediately.

(ii) **Care of withdrawal symptoms :** A drug has the tendency to produce withdrawal symptoms either psychological or physical which are treated by giving medicines like analgesics, antiemetics, multivitamins depending on the condition.

(iii) **Rehabilitation :** This is a part of the long treatment for those patients who need moral support and psychotherapy particularly victims of narcotic drugs or alcohol. A self-help group like narcotic Anonymous, Alcohol Anonymous may help.

(iv) Government support : It is not a part of the direct treatment but by controlling the traffic of drugs (Narcotics) under the narcotic Drugs and spychtropic substances Act - 1985 can stop the population from getting addicted.

Commonly Abused drug :

The drugs of abuse are categorised as follows :

1. **Narcotics :** Opiates (Morphin, Heroin pethidene).
2. **CNS depressants :** Alcohol, Barbiturates, sedatives.
3. **CNS stimulants :** Tobacco, caffeine cocaine.
4. **Hallucinogens :** LSD, cannabis.
5. **Inhalants :** Hydrocarbons (Acetone, Petrol, Benzene).

1. Opiates :

This class of drugs are very commonly used by the addict persons. Heroin and brown-sugar are choice of drugs. A dose of 25 mg of heroin's effect lasts for about four hours. So repeated administration is needed to avoid psychological and physical discomfort.

Medical complications : The abuse of opiates results in a syndrome like constipation, excitement, drowsiness, swelling of hands and feet, pin point pupils, impotence in male. There are chances of Hepatitis and AIDS due to use of contaminated needles.

Withdrawal symptoms : Sudden stoppage of morphine or heroin shows withdrawal syndrome which varies with person to person. The abstinence symptoms begin after 8 hrs of the last dose and last for a couple of months. The stages are summarized as under :

After 8 hours : Yawning, anxiety, sweating, crying and rhinorrhoea.

At 20 hours : Chills and panicness.

24 to 48 hours : Nausia, vomiting, diarrhoea, hypertension, which may lead to fever.

Up to 1 week : Severe muscle cramps.

Week to months : Sleep disturbances (Insomnia) and anxiety.

Treatment : The purpose of the treatment is not only to secure the patient but to obtain complete abstinence of drug. It involves.

(a) **Pharmacological approach :** A narcotic antagonist like naltrexone is given orally. It blocks the action of opiates.

A substitute like methadone at a dose of 30 mg in divided dosage is given for initial 3 days. Then the dose is reduced to 10 mg/day.

(b) **Psychological approach :** Apart from the drug treatment, moral and social counselling is desirable in such conditions.

2. Hallucinogens :

Some groups of drugs produce hallucination. It is a state in which perception of matters with no reality or feeling with no external cause; and other alterations of mood like illusion, delusion, ideation etc. are observed by the effect of such drugs.

Other terms are used for hallucinogens are :

(a) **Psychometric :** Means the actions produced are resembling with those observed in natural psychoses e.g. cannabis.

(b) **Psychedelics : (Mind revealing)** The drug causes marked changes in perception, judgment or mood e.g. LSD (Lysergic acid diethyamide) scopolamine, ketamine and harmaline.

(i) Cannabis :

Cannabis sativa is obtained from hemp plant. It is available in various forms viz.

- **Hashish / Charas :** Dried exudate obtained from flowering tops.
- **Ganja :** A resinous mass obtained from leaves.
- **Bhang :** Active substance obtained from dried leaf flowering shoots.
- **Marijuana :** It is an extract of the plant or any chopped part of plant.

Symptoms : Starts within few minutes after consuming the dose.

1. Feeling of drowsiness and floating.

2. Feeling of dancing nude women in front of him.
3. Wrong perceptions of sound, colours etc.
4. Memory impairment for short duration.
5. Confusion and in-co-ordination.
6. Psychotic behaviours may occur.

Treatment : A supportive environment is needed. Antianxiety and tranquilizers like Diazepam are given.

3. Alcohol :

Alcohol is consumed by the community for a variety and reasons either to experience euphoria, alleviate anxiety, or on social ground as part of living style.

A chronic consumption of alcohol results in increased capacity to metabolise it. The metabolize process declines or stops after a period time. This results into tolerance and higher concentration of alcohol is needed.

Medical complications :
(i) Decrease in appetite
(ii) Gastric disturbances
(iii) Hepatic complications
(iv) Hypoglycemia
(v) Convulsive disorders.

Withdrawal symptoms :

The symptoms start after about 6-8 hours and stopping the dose of alcohol ranging from hangover to delirium.

After 6-8 hours : Headache, sweating, tachycardia, muscle twitch, insomnia.

After 2-3 days : Dis - Orientation, hallucination, seizures.

Treatment :
(i) Sedatives like Diazepam.
(ii) Disulfiram in a dose of 0.5 gm/day.
(iii) Thiamine for nutritional disturbances.

QUESTIONS

1. Define the terms :

    (i) Drug abuse [S - 99, W - 97]

    (ii) Drug habituation [S - 99, 00 : W - 96, 97, 99, 07]

    (iii) Drug. dependence [S - 96 : W - 96]

2. Differentiate Drug Addiction and Habituation [(S - 03, 99) 4 marks]

3. Differentiate between psychological and physical drug dependence.

    [(S - 01, 97) 4 marks]

4. Give the treatment of drug abuse. [W - 03]

5. What are the reasons of drug abuse ? How drug addicts are treated ? [W - 99]

6. Write a note on Hallucination. [S - 02]

7. What is drug addiction ? Name any 3 drugs which cause it. How it is treated ? [(S - 01 : W - 02) 4 marks]

■■■

10

BIOAVAILABILITY OF DRUGS

(Blood Serum Drug Level)

INTRODUCTION

This is essential to understand the way in which a drug is absorbed after administration. The route by which the drug is given, determines the latent period between administration time and it's effect. There are few drugs which are inactivated by certain factors like enzymatic degradation (e.g. Insulin), poor absorption from GIT (e.g. streptomycin) and during first pass via liver (e.g. aldosterone and testosterone).

The pharmaceutical formulation does not produce the same physical and chemical quantitative results in vivo after it's absorption : as shown at the time of vitro testing performed as per official standards laid down in pharmacopoeia.

Bioavailability is defined as the fraction or percentage amount of drug that is absorbed from the given dosage that reaches to the systemic circulation.

When the drug is given by intravenous route of administration, the bioavailability is 100% and called **absolute bioavailability**.

Bioequivalance, means a product does not show a significant difference in its rate and extent of systemic absorption from pioneer drug product when administered at the same dose, route and experiment conditions.

According to the US FDA (1973) definition it is difficult to measure the availability and drug at the site of action. Indirectly it is measured by the pharmacological effect produced by the drug.

The concentration of drug at the receptor sites and in circulation totally depends upon the pharmacokinetic of the drug. i.e. Absorption, distribution, metabolism and elimination.

Process of Absorption :

It is essential to know the way in which a drug absorbed from GIT. The actual mechanism of absorption is very complex phenomenon, but it occurs through the passage of drug across cell membrane either directly or indirectly, which is governed by the lipid barrier present at cell membrane. The ways by which the drug absorbed are as :

1. Passive diffusion : It is also known as simple diffusion because it takes place without utilising the energy, but the concentration gradient across cell membrane governed the rate of absorption. Both, fat soluble and water soluble molecules of small size cross the cell membrane via pores present in the membrane.

2. Active transport : It is a unique process, where involvement of carrier molecule with utilization of energy takes place. The carrier molecule combines with the drug which depends upon the physical properties of drug molecule to form a complex on one side of cell membrane. The formed complex the diffuses through membrane and dissociate when it reaches the other side of membrane as carrier molecule and drug. Later the carrier returns to the original side and the cycle continues.

Factors affecting Drug Absorption and Bioavailablity :

There are numerous factors which affect the rate of absorption and bio-availability of drug they are :

1. **Physical properties of the drug :** Solubility is an important criteria of absorption for a drug through gastrointestinal tract. Water soluble drugs are easily absorbed from stomach rather than oily form. Bile helps in absorbing oil soluble vitamins like A, D, K, E via small intestine.

2. **Pharmaceutical aspects :** The additives added and the process of fabrication by different manufactures for the same drug and dosage form shows variations in rate of absorption and bioavailability; due to the following reasons.

    (a) **Additives :** Diluent like lactose, dicalcium phosphate, cellulose and other excipients like binders, lubricants alter the rate of disintegration and dissolution time.

    (b) **Disintegration and Dissolution time :** Disintegration rate is a gauge, which measures the rate of break up the tablet or capsule into the granule, while the dissolution means, time needed for the drug to go into the solution form.

    In both of these the rate and time varies for manufactures to the same drug and dosage form. Therefore, absorption and bioavailability are altered.

(c) Nature of Formation : The drug, formulated in various dosage form, has to undergo a number of stages to reach the systemic circulation it is demonstrated as given below.

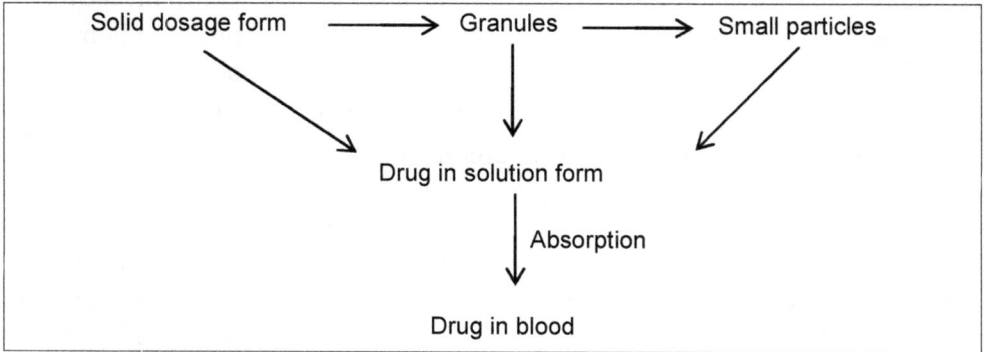

This suggests that the rate and absorption and bioavailability of drug from different dosage forms in general can be in the following order.

Solution : > Suspension > Powder > Capsule > Tablet.

(d) Particle size : The above order clears that sparingly soluble drugs like chloramphenicol and carticosteroid's solubility can be increased by doing as possible as small particle size.

3. **Physiological Factors :** Like above discussed factors physiology and associated organ function also affect absorption and bioavailability.

   (a) pH of Gastrointestinal tract : The weekly acidic and basic drugs exist in two forms i.e. an unionised form and an ionised component. An ionised form is water soluble and is poorly absorbed; but an unionised drug can cross the cell membrane which contains lipids; because of solubility.

   Acidic drugs like **salicylates** are rapidly absorbed from the stomach because the drug remains in an unionised form which favours its absorption.

   Basic drugs are absorbed only when they reaches the small intestine because of alkaline environment and the drug fraction exists in an unionised state e.g. pithidine.

   (b) Gastrointestinal transit time : The presence of food material, viscosity and motility of intestine affects the absorption of drug defained time.

   For example, absorption of ampicilline, tetracyclines is reduced in the presence of food.

   While Ach. increase rate of motility, results in decrease in the stay if drug in GIT and affect absorption and bioavailability.

(c) **Presence of other Agents :** There are few drugs which favour and reduces the absorption of other drugs.

For example : Absorption of iron is increased by Vitamin C while liquid paraffin reduces absorption of fat soluble Vitamin viz. A, D, E, K.

(d) **First pass :** First pass means the drug degradation occurs before it reaches the systemic circulation. The net result is decreased bioavailability, that diminishes therapeutic response. This happens to all the drugs taken orally, after absorption through GIT; it goes first to Hepatic (Portal) circulation, where first pass takes place by liver.

4. **Genetic Factors :** It is related with genetically mediated variations in drug response; due to defective enzyme systems, which involves in activating drugs. A microsomal enzyme system plays an important role in **metabolism** of the drug.

   For example : An individual who lacks an enzyme, Glucose-6-phosphate dehydrogenase, shows adverse effects to primaquine.

5. **Disease State :** Diseases like diarrhoea, vomiting, malabsorption, thyrotouicosx and liver destruction like cirrhosis and bilary obstruction affects the absorption and bioavailability of the drug.

QUESTIONS

1. Define Bioavailability of drug. [W - 00]
2. Define the term Bioavailability and name the factors affecting it.

   [S - 97, W - 02 and S - 03]

3. Explain the role of Biological factors that control bioavailability. [S - 04]

   OR

   Explain, How physiological factors influence or affect the bio-availability.

4. Discuss the pharmaceutical factors which affect the bioavailability of drug.

   [(W – 97, 03, 02, 01, 99, 97)]

5. Discuss the physical properties of drugs which affect their bioavailability.

   [S - 04, 03, 02, 01, 97, 96]

■■■

www.ingramcontent.com/pod-product-compliance
Lightning Source LLC
Chambersburg PA
CBHW081919170426
43200CB00014B/2764